D0038725

Contents

PLEASE . . . With the exception of the Frank Lloyd Wright Home & Studio and Unity Temple, the tour buildings described here are private residences and are not open to the public. Please respect the privacy of the residents and their property and environment. Individuals interested in obtaining further information on specific buildings or guided tour programs may contact the Oak Park Visitors Center (708) 848-1500.

Acknowledgements

This book has been made possible through the generosity of a great many individuals and organizations. The Oak Park Bicentennial and Landmarks Commissions, Village of Oak Park, gratefully acknowledge the assistance of:

The Historical Society of Oak Park and River Forest
GreatAmerican Federal Savings
St. Paul Federal Bank for Savings
Oak Park Trust and Savings Bank
Avenue Bank & Trust Company of Oak Park
The Citizens of Oak Park

Also, we wish to note the following:

This project is funded in part by a grant from the Illinois Arts Council, a state agency, as part of their Bicentennial Project ILLINOIS ARCHITECTURE: REVOLUTION ON THE PRAIRIE.

The cover design is taken from the laminated oak ceiling grille in the 1895 dining room of the Frank Lloyd Wright Home in Oak Park.
Design courtesy of the Frank Lloyd Wright Home and Studio Foundation.

GUIDE TO FRANK LLOYD WRIGHT & PRAIRIE SCHOOL ARCHITECTURE IN OAK PARK □□ PAUL E. SPRAGUE

Fifth Edition

Oak Park Bicentennial Commission
of the American Revolution
Oak Park Landmarks Commission
Village of Oak Park
Oak Park, Illinois 60302

Acknowledgements

**Photographs
and Assistance**

Elmer Roberts
Ruth Van Bergen
Roger White
Lloyd Wright
Mrs. Frederick K. Wykes

Tory Bruno
Wilbert R. Hasbrouck
Donald Kalec
John Michiels
John J. Mojonnier, Jr.
Oak Park and River Forest High School
Marcia Palazzolo
Sturr-Young Ltd.

Burnham Library of Architecture
Chicago Public Library
John Crerar Library
Oak Park Public Library
Park District of Oak Park

E. E. Roberts Architectural Preservation Society
Frank Lloyd Wright Home & Studio Foundation
The Historical Society of Oak Park and River Forest

Fifth Edition

Library of Congress Catalog Card No.: 86-50596
ISBN 0-9616915-0-6

Foreword

Oak Park has long enjoyed an international reputation for its architecture. Primarily this is due to the many Frank Lloyd Wright buildings located here, but also to the splendid ensemble of homes, many of them designed by Wright's contemporaries among the architects of the Prairie School. The ideals expressed in these buildings have exercised a world-wide influence which continues to abound.

Frank Lloyd Wright was one of the world's greatest architects, the only one who was an American, and the only one to focus his genius upon the crucial problem of the family home. For twenty years (1889-1909) — the most significant and influential in his long productive life (b.1867-d.1959) — he lived and worked in Oak Park where he built his home and studio (which, today, are open to the public).

The Prairie School had its beginnings in the 1890s, and although its impetus was largely spent by the first World War, its impact was profound. Representing a generation of architects born from the 1860s to '80s, and including (among others) Wright, Walter Griffin, Marion Mahony, William Purcell, George Elmslie, Barry Byrne, Robert Spencer, William Drummond, George Maher, Thomas Tallmadge, Vernon Watson, John Van Bergen, and Louis Sullivan in his later years, it was probably the most thoroughly American architectural expression this country has ever known. Stemming from the philosophical writings of Emerson, Thoreau, and Whitman, and deriving, in part, from local traditions in vernacular building, it was uniquely American both in its manifestation and its point of view. It celebrated the landscape in the setting and repose of its buildings, reflected the openness of the prairie and the endless expansion of continent in its interior planning, exalted natural materials and the machine whose processing enhanced their usefulness and beauty, and honored the abstract pattern of structure itself rather than historical forms or self-conscious ornamentation. It was conservative yet revolutionary, manifestly American yet universal in its ideals. At the popular level it helped inspire the recent craze for ranch-style homes, at its most profound it offers a timeless (but often ill-understood) example of how we and future generations, confronted with soaring building costs and ever smaller apartments and homes, can obtain more effective planning and enjoy a new sense of spaciousness which the actual size of our homes would seem to deny.

These buildings are an incredible heritage, each in its own way, and even the least of them helps lend to the tree lined streets of Oak Park, a character which is special as an urban, or suburban, scene.

H. Allen Brooks
Department of Fine Art
University of Toronto

July 3, 1975 . . . Toronto, Canada

This guide is the result of intensive research extending over more than a decade. Although in a work of this kind it is not possible to cite sources, documentation does exist for all entries. Notes of special interest, indicated by italics, have been prepared by the Guidebook Committee.

Lest the reader be misled, he is forewarned that the buildings by the Prairie Architects presented in this guide represent only a selection of their work in Oak Park. Although the guide includes the most interesting buildings by these architects, it does not pretend to be comprehensive.

An excellent overall study of Prairie Architecture is The Prairie School: Frank Lloyd Wright and His Midwest Contemporaries *by H. Allen Brooks. A comprehensive listing of architecturally significant Oak Park buildings is contained in the* Hasbrouck-Sprague Survey of Historic Architecture in Oak Park, *available at the Oak Park Public Library and some book stores. The Oak Park Public Library is a particularly rich source of books, publications, and reference materials on Frank Lloyd Wright and other Prairie Architects.*

The first edition of this Guide appeared on July 4, 1976. A guide had long been a dream of Oak Park's Landmarks Commission; it became a reality through cooperation with Oak Park's Bicentennial Commission of the American Revolution. Fittingly, the Guide appeared on the anniversary of our Declaration of Independence.

Members of the two commissions formed a Guidebook Committee consisting of Robert A. Bell, Redd Griffin, Frank A. Tuma, Morris R. Buske (Bicentennial Chairman), and Roy G. Hlavacek (Landmarks Chairman and Chairman of the Committee). When the Bicentennial Commission finished its term, it asked that receipts from guidebook sales go to promote Oak Park's architectural heritage, with the funds to be administered by the Landmarks Commission. This has been done.

The Guide was received enthusiastically by visitors to Oak Park and by Oak Parkers themselves, many of whom had not fully appreciated the architectural treasures of their village.

By 1978 depleted supplies of the Guide made a second edition necessary. Careful re-thinking shaped the new edition; over half of the pages contained one or more changes. A third edition in 1982 carried minor corrections.

This, the fourth edition, is the result of further study. Contact has been made with owners of practically all the buildings pictured on these pages, to make sure that statements herein are factual. Continuing demand for the Guide caused this printing to be the largest to date.

Special recognition and credit for the fourth edition should go especially to Carol R. Kelm, Landmarks Commission member and Curator for the Historical Society of Oak Park and River Forest. Her efforts were ably assisted by Landmarks Commissioner Margaret Klinkow in field follow up. We are also grateful to Commissioner James Groll for his excellent new cover design and guidebook production coordination.

Oak Park, Illinois, June 1986   John J. Mojonnier, Jr., Chairman
                                     Landmarks Commission

INTRODUCTION TO PRAIRIE ARCHITECTURE

The term "Prairie School" refers to a group of architects working in the Chicago metropolitan area between 1890 and 1917 who shared the common ideal of producing an original style of architecture.

In driving forward towards a new style, the Prairie architects were rejecting, in the process, the idea that new buildings should be inspired by or derived from the historic styles of architecture. They rejected the historic styles because they, like many of their predecessors in the nineteenth-century, believed themselves to be living in a new cultural age whose architecture deserved an aesthetic expression of its own. To their way of thinking, each historic style had arisen mystically out of what they referred to as "the spirit" of its own time and place. Such styles, representing the ideals and convictions of bygone cultures, ought not, in their judgment, be imposed on modern civilization. Thus the Prairie architects, like their radical European counterparts, set out to eliminate from their own work all vestiges of historic architecture.

But in exorcizing the "costume" of historic buildings from their work, the Prairie architects did not also cast aside the principles of composition and planning that have always transcended historic periods and styles. Thus, some Prairie architects preferred formal or symmetrical compositions while others emphasized irregular and picturesque arrangements. Wright, for example, often introduced formal or symmetrical components as parts of his normally asymmetrical or informal schemes. Yet his non-residentail designs, such as Unity Temple, were invariably organized formally. Therefore, when viewing buildings by the Prairie architects, we will normally find them free of the stylistic trappings of historic architecture, but planned and composed according to those universal principles of design that, in greater or lesser degree, have served the architect throughout history, whatever the style or aesthetic qualities of his architecture.

What are the visual elements that give unity to the work of this group of midwestern architects? Like so much later modern architecture in Europe and America, the architectural style they created was based on the reduction of architectural masses, shapes, and details to their most essential forms: cubes and other rectangular and polygonal solids; squares, rectangles, triangles, and circles; flat surfaces and straight lines. Architectural ornament in their hands became either stylized floral abstractions or else complicated geometric patterns. It was thus abstract geometry of a generally rectilinear sort — plus

7

stylized representations of botanical types — that served to unite the work of these architects and, at the same time, provided each of them with a basis from which to evolve his own special brand of Prairie architecture.

The goal of the Prairie architects was visual and artistic only. Do not be misled by the myths that say they were attempting to invent new architectural forms suitable for machine fabrication or that they were trying to give expression to the new materials or processes of the machine age. In their work they employed both traditional and modern materials and structural systems and bent all of them to their visual and aesthetic aims.

If we are to appreciate the achievement of these architects, another myth that must be put aside is that they evolved an architectural style expressing

5. Frank Lloyd Wright Home

the horizontality and flatness of the American prairie. Although it is true that Wright himself often voiced this idea, which seems to find expression in many of his buildings as well as those by other Prairie architects, the concept is a limited one which does not apply generally either to Wright's buildings or to those by the other Prairie architects. The original style these architects achieved did not owe its origin to the visual qualities of the landscape in which America's second city is set.

Originally these architects were known collectively as the "Chicago School," a far better term for them because it does not bring to mind any visual or stylistic attributes as does the term "Prairie School." Unfortunately for this movement, the name "Chicago School" later gained currency as appellation for a group of architects, of mixed and often contradictory ideals, who, in designing the large commercial buildings of Chicago's Loop, would sometimes, though rarely, shed the mantle of the historic styles.

Louis Sullivan, whose commercial architecture in Chicago and elsewhere after 1889 was largely free of the paraphernalia of historic architecture has been associated with both groups. Though included in the Chicago School by historical accident rather than by intention, it is Sullivan's role as inventor of the first modern architectural style in America and as a leader of a younger group of radical architects that assures him an esteemed position in American cultural history. Accordingly, it was Sullivan, not Wright, who "founded" the Prairie School of Architecture as the term is used here.

In his first mature works, the Getty Tomb in Chicago and the Wainwright Building in St. Louis, both designed in 1890, Sullivan achieved the goal of a modern style by largely ignoring the precedents of historic buildings. Instead he based their masses, shapes and details on the abstract forms of plane and

24. John Farson House

66. Henry D. Golbeck House

25. Flori Blondeel I

solid geometry. His architectural ornament, by contrast, was based both on geometric shapes and stylized plants. In keeping with his academic American and French training, Sullivan's modern style was one of monumentality in composition and formality in planning.

To his more famous pupil, Frank Lloyd Wright, Sullivan passed on this ideal of a modern style of architecture as well as the essential ingredients of the style he had invented. It was to be Wright's role to synthesize the formality of Sullivan's new style with the informal aspects, in materials, planning, and composition, of the "picturesque" historic styles that Wright learned from his first teacher, Joseph L. Silsbee.

It is the qualities of irregularity and complexity in planning and composition, all quite foreign to Sullivan's architecture, that give Wright's buildings their pictureque quality and dynamic interior spatial characteristics.

9

The organic overtones which make Wright's buildings, especially residences, appear to blend into and become one with nature and the land come from the same sources. This is in opposition to the formal architecture of Sullivan, which stands on the land in geometric and monumental detachment.

The organic qualities of Wright's architecture were also attained by the use of rough materials such as boulders, bricks with mottled surfaces, concrete containing a pebble aggregate, and sand-finished stucco and plaster. To the same end Wright used rough-sawn lumber, not finished by planing or dressing, natural woods preserved only by staining, oiling or waxing, and autumnal color schemes of delicate browns, light greens and golden yellows. His stained glass windows, marked at first by small squares of white and gold, and later by the irridescent pinks, greens and blues of Tiffany, also become an important part of the organic ensemble, dissolving the surfaces of his windows into a rich texture of colored and clear reflections.

These organic qualities of irregularity in planning and composition, of varied and often rough surface textures, and of color schemes derived from nature and from materials used in their natural state, were transmitted to Wright by Silsbee from a "picturesque" tradition in architecture and landscape planning going back at least to the eighteenth century. This organic romanticism which characterizes most of Wright's buildings is associated with certain American architectural styles of the 1880s through 1900s, especially the Queen Anne and the Romanesque styles.

It was not until 1897 that Wright began to evolve a personal style of his own. The development of that style continued until 1900 when, in two houses built at Kankakee, Illinois, Wright attained his goal. Paying homage to both Silsbee and Sullivan, Wright's first modern or Prairie style was the mixture of organic and geometric elements that we associate with his twentieth-century architecture in Oak Park. During the early years of this century Wright designed building after building in this "Oak Park style" executed in wood, stucco, brick and stone, and concrete. Not until 1913 did he finally lose interest in his Prairie manner. In that year Wright designed the famous Midway Gardens in Chicago in a new expressionistic style that was to carry him through his Japanese and California periods.

In addition to Sullivan (1856-1924) and Wright (1867-1959), the Prairie School included two distinct groups of architects. The first were inspired by Sullivan and Wright to seek a modern style and the second were actually trained in the offices of the two leaders. Of the Prairie architects who built in Oak Park, four belonged to the first group, two to the second.

Like Wright, George W. Maher (1864-1926) had received his training from Joseph Silsbee, but the formal qualities of his mature architecture seem to be inspired by Sullivan, for whom he never worked. That he had not been forcibly exposed to Sullivan's ideology and artistic discipline may partly explain why Maher's version of Prairie architecture is so individualistic and often marked by idiosyncratic effects and details. In general, Maher's architecture tends to be monumental and dignified. His walls are generally more continuous and without the variations and complexities of surface detail that enliven Wright's buildings.

Wright's close friend, Robert Spencer (1864-1953), who lived in neighboring River Forest and published the first article about Wright's work in 1900, gradually evolved a modern style of his own under the influence of Sullivan and Wright. So far as exteriors are concerned, Spencer's mature Prairie architecture resembles Wright's but is generally less complex in its massing and details. After 1905 he practiced with Horace Powers as Spencer & Powers.

In 1905 Vernon Watson (1878-1950) formed a partnership with Evanston architect Thomas Tallmadge. He was a gifted designer with a flair for capturing the geometric essence of Sullivan's and Wright's work and re-combining their forms and details into a wide range of stylistic variations. He and his partner built many houses in Oak Park before the first world war, almost all of them unmistakably cast in the Prairie idiom.

Eben E. Roberts (1866-1943) was a popular Oak Park architect who adapted the radical architectural elements of Wright, Maher, and Sullivan into

10. *Interior of E. E. Roberts House*

a popular residential and commercial Prairie style. In 1903 he began to design symmetrical stucco houses with full-width front porches that have a sharp-edged geometry which gives them a distinct Prairie cast. That Roberts had been inspired by the examples of Wright, Maher, and Sullivan to find a modern style of his own seems obvious, but lacking a proper background for understanding the aims of these leaders, his version of Prairie architecture is sometimes contradictory and often highly eclectic.

The other two Prairie architects working in Oak Park were both students of Wright. John S. Van Bergen (1885-1969) had, in fact, worked not only for Wright, but also for two of Wright's chief draftsmen, Walter Griffin and William Drummond, before entering private practice in 1911. As might be

11

expected under those circumstances, his independent work is extremely reminiscent of Wright's version of Prairie architecture.

Whether Charles E. White Jr. (1876-1936) should be classed as a student of Wright's is debatable since he already had worked as an architect for a number of years before joining Wright's office in 1903. Yet White's early independent work in Oak Park, as exemplified by the small stucco residences he designed between 1905 and 1910, their plain walls punctured here and there by casement windows and sometimes softened by curved and sloping surfaces, are certainly without historic pretense and thus are modern. But they appear to be modern in an English sense rather than in the Prairie School manner.

The American proponents of historic architecture were not easily dissuaded from their point of view. In fact, after the turn of the century they

38. Herman W. Mallen House   3. Charles E. Matthews House

gradually succeeded in converting the public to their way of thinking. By World War I they so completely ruled the field, even in the Midwest, that the Prairie architects found it exceedingly difficult to find clients for their modern style. Many of the Prairie architects simply left and began designing in the historic styles. Others gave up independent practice altogether. Only the more dedicated survived by sheer persistence, though none of them very successfully.

Sullivan died in poverty in 1924. Wright stayed afloat by going west to California and Japan. After the first world war, Van Bergen somehow managed to find a limited market for his modern style in Chicago's North Shore suburbs. Robert Spencer built little after the war and finally left Chicago to teach architecture. Vernon Watson, Charles White, George Maher and Eben Roberts turned to designing in the historic styles.

Given so dismal an ending for this first era of modern architecture, one may well wonder why the buildings of these architects in Oak Park and elsewhere are so esteemed today. The answer must be sought in two realms, one, the fine arts, and the other, cultural history.

Several of the Prairie architects were extraordinary artists. Buildings by Sullivan and Wright would be revered today even if they had chosen to work in the traditional historic styles, in much the same way that the historically reminiscent buildings of Henry H. Richardson are still so loved and respected. Many of the lesser Prairie architects were first-rate designers and, again, it is likely their work would also be sought out today even if cast in the historic styles.

Thus one might answer the question in part by saying that, before anything else, the buildings by the Prairie architects, and especially by the most artistic among them, interest us because they are exceptional works of art. In this light, Oak Park becomes a rich and impressive outdoor art gallery.

Equally important is the significant historical position occupied by the Prairie architects. Here, in the Chicago metropolitan area, arose the first and, except for the work of a few California architects, only truly American style of modern architecture. It is in the relatively few buildings bequeathed to us by this small band of visionaries, that we have the eloquent visual record of their unsuccessful struggle to change the course of American architecture. That they failed in their aim does not diminish in the least the value of their work both aesthetically and historically as a distinguished part of America's cultural patrimony.

As the artistic and cultural values of Prairie architecture are thus accorded proper recognition, is it any wonder that the work of these midwestern architects receives such ardent international acclaim? Or is it at all surprising that so much attention has been focused on the Village of Oak Park with its extensive collection of buildings by Frank Lloyd Wright, his colleagues, contemporaries and students? Surely there can be no question that, so long as these famous buildings stand, they will continue to be regarded with pride and respect by the nation, and sought out as sacred shrines by architectural pilgrims from the world over.

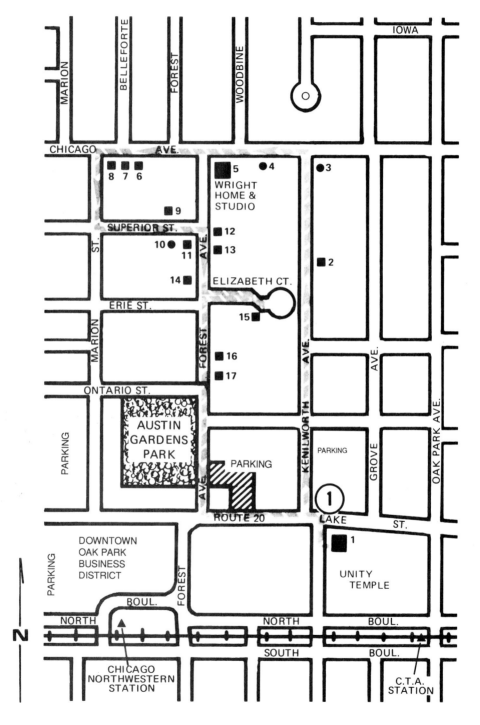

FOREST AVENUE — TOUR 1

Approximate Walking Time: one hour, ten minutes

1.	Unity Temple — 1905-8 *F. L. Wright*	Lake at Kenilworth
2.	H. P. Young House — 1895, *F. L. Wright*	334 N. Kenilworth
3.	Charles E. Matthews House — 1909, *Tallmadge & Watson*	432 N. Kenilworth
4.	H. Benton Howard House — 1903-4, *E. E. Roberts*	911 Chicago
5.	Frank Lloyd Wright House — 1889-95, *F. L. Wright*	428 Forest
	Frank Lloyd Wright Studio — 1898, *F. L. Wright*	951 Chicago
6.	Robert P. Parker House — 1892, *F. L. Wright*	1019 Chicago
7.	Thomas H. Gale House — 1892, *F. L. Wright*	1027 Chicago
8.	Walter H. Gale House — 1893, *F. L. Wright*	1031 Chicago
9.	Francis J. Woolley House — 1893, *F. L. Wright*	1030 Superior
10.	Eben Ezra Roberts House — 1911, *E. E. Roberts*	1019 Superior
11.	Nathan G. Moore House — 1895/1923, *F. L. Wright*	333 Forest
12.	Dr. William H. Copeland House — 1908-9, *F. L. Wright*	400 Forest
13.	Arthur Heurtley House — 1902, *F. L. Wright*	318 Forest
14.	Edward R. Hills House — 1906, *F. L. Wright*	313 Forest
15.	Mrs. Thomas H. Gale House — 1909, *F. L. Wright*	6 Elizabeth
16.	Peter A. Beachy House — 1906, *F. L. Wright*	238 Forest
17.	Frank W. Thomas House — 1901, *F. L. Wright*	210 Forest

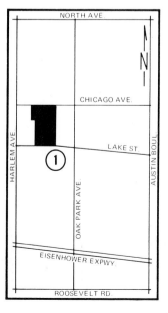

PLEASE . . . With the exception of the Frank Lloyd Wright Home & Studio and Unity Temple, the tour buildings described here are private residences and are not open to the public. Please respect the privacy of the residents and their property and environment. Individuals interested in obtaining further information on specific buildings or guided tour programs may contact the Oak Park Visitors Center (708) 848-1500.

The Unitarian Universalist Church building, declared a National Historic Landmark in 1969, has been carefully restored. It is open daily for tours. Contact the Oak Park Visitors Center (708) 848-1500 for details.

1. Unity Temple
Lake Street at Kenilworth Avenue
Frank Lloyd Wright
1905-8

In its outwardly simple sculptural forms, this three-dimensional monument to "the worship of God and the service of man" may seem much less complicated than it really is. That Wright could thus endow this impressive composition with so strong a sense of repose, while yet constructing it out of a series of complexly interlocking rectilinear solids, is a testimony to his extraordinary gift as a three-dimensional artist. In this respect, Wright far exceeded the abilities of his teacher, Louis Sullivan, even though it is to Sullivan's commercial work that the abstract geometric masses of Unity Temple must ultimately be traced.

Begun in 1906, but not finished until 1908, this religious complex of church and parish house was constructed throughout of reinforced concrete. To soften the harshness of the concrete, its pebble aggregate was exposed by scrubbing and washing the exterior after the forms were removed. The interior walls were subdivided and accentuated by strips of hardwood, and their plaster surfaces painted in browns, light greens and yellows.

Interior of Unity Temple on November 9, 1974 during ceremonies marking the listing of the Frank Lloyd Wright—Prairie School of Architecture Historic District in the National Register of Historic Places. Program speakers included Paul E. Sprague (seated) and Wilbert R. Hasbrouck (standing).

The church proper is a simple cubic volume of space lighted from above by a skylight and clerestory windows of art glass. Its balconies, passageways, and other subsidiary spaces serve, however, to enlarge and expand this central well of space into a highly complex volume. Wright deliberately placed the lectern of this liberal church against the entry wall so that the congregation would depart by walking toward the minister instead of away from him.

2. H. P. Young House Remodeling
334 N. Kenilworth Avenue
Frank Lloyd Wright
1895

With its high-pitched gable roofs, pointed windows in the attic, diamond-pane glass and other historic details, the house recalls domestic architecture of the late Middle Ages in England. The client, H. P. Young, worked as a purchasing agent. Wright's ambitious 1895 designs for Nathan Moore's Medieval Revival house (No. 11) may have influenced the remodeling and enlarging of Young's house.

Wright either added or else totally remodeled the front two-thirds of the house. A part of Young's original home may still be seen on the south side just beyond the bay window. The sharply rectilinear chimney of Roman brick, second floor casement windows grouped together, and the cantilevered carriage entrance roof look ahead to the architecture of Wright's maturity.

3. Charles E. Matthews House
432 N. Kenilworth Avenue
Tallmadge & Watson
1909

No doubt it was the architecture of George Maher that inspired Tallmadge & Watson to design this very formal all-stucco house. The Maher-like simplicity accorded its masses and surfaces enabled the architects to concentrate their decorative talents on the ornamentation of the monumental story-and-a-half entrance pavilion. That the owner, Charles Matthews (1860-1945), was sufficiently affluent to afford so artistic a house, testifies to the degree of his success in the drug industry.

3. *Charles E. Matthews House*

4. H. Benton Howard House
911 Chicago Avenue
Eben E. Roberts
1903-4

Designed in 1903 by Eben Roberts, the house was built by Americus B. Melville as a gift to his daughter and her husband. Melville erected his own larger house next to it at the corner of Kenilworth and Chicago Avenues in 1904, also from designs by Roberts. Although still exhibiting the varied materials and shapes that marked Roberts' earlier Queen Anne houses, the Howard House clearly demonstrates in its cubic masses, linear emphasis, low hip roofs, and geometric ornament, Roberts' awareness of the architecture of Frank Lloyd Wright.

5. Frank Lloyd Wright House
428 Forest Avenue
Frank Lloyd Wright
1889

Playroom and Dining Room Additions
1895

Wright began this small residence in 1889 shortly after his marriage to Catherine Tobin. It was here that he lived during his first twenty years of architectural practice while designing the now-famous buildings of his Oak Park period. Originally the room at the front of the house on the second floor served as his drafting room until his studio building was finished in 1898 on Chicago Avenue.

In 1895 he added the the two-story polygonal bay onto the south side. It contained a new dining room on the ground floor and above it, an enlarged bedroom.

In 1895 he also added a two-story structure onto the rear of the house. Occupying its ground floor was a new kitchen and a maid's room. Over them Wright built the superb vaulted room that was to serve as his children's playroom. This splendid space, illuminated on both sides by art-glass windows, also received light from above through a skylight shielded from view by exquisite screens of fret-sawed wood.

When Wright remodeled the house as a rental unit in 1911, he changed the house significantly by adding a porch and moving the main entrance to the south side. The house has been restored to the way it was in 1909 — the last time that Wright and his family lived here.

Frank Lloyd Wright Studio
951 Chicago Avenue
Frank Lloyd Wright
1898

Adjoining Wright's house on the north is a brick-and-shingle building that he designed in 1898 to serve as his architectural office. A large portion of the funds for its erection came from a commission of 1897 from the Luxfer Prism Company in connection with a promotional competition calling attention to their newly-developed electro-glazed illuminating prisms.

When finished in 1898, the studio consisted of a low entrance pavilion connecting an octagonal library on the right with a two-story drafting room on the left. Wright's private office was located directly behind the reception hall. Over the years Wright gradually remodeled the building. The most drastic changes came in 1911 when Wright remodeled the studio into living space for his family who then moved here from the Forest Avenue home. The studio has been restored to its 1909 appearance — the last time Wright used the building as his work space.

A wide flight of steps leads from Chicago Avenue past brick piers into the reception hall. The drafting room consists of a square first floor of bricks and shingles and an octagonal second story covered with boards and battens laid horizontally. Inside, the two-story space is open to a pitched octagonal ceiling 27 feet above the floor. An encircling balcony is suspended from the roof beams on chains. The library is also covered by an octagonal roof of low pitch that is mostly a skylight.

This picturesque group of buildings, now commonly kown as "The Frank Lloyd Wright Home and Studio," was declared a National Historic Landmark in 1975. A major restoration program for the buildings has been completed by the Frank Lloyd Wright Home and Studio Foundation, a non-profit organization. The Home and Studio has guided tours throughout the year which start in the Ginkgo Tree Bookshop off Chicago Avenue.

21

6. Robert P. Parker House
1019 Chicago Avenue
Frank Lloyd Wright
1892

7. Thomas H. Gale House
1027 Chicago Avenue
Frank Lloyd Wright
1892

Wright's plans for these nearly identical houses were derived from the more expensive residence he had designed earlier in 1892 for Robert Emmond of La Grange, Illinois. They were built later that same year by realtor Thomas Gale who occupied the one at 1027 and sold the other, at 1019, to attorney Robert Parker.

In spite of their small size and inexpensive detailing, these houses are of interest for what they tell us about Wright's artistic development. In their irregular composition, consisting of octagonal bays joined to a rectangular core, the whole covered by high-pitched roofs with polygonal dormers, we are reminded of Wright's debt to the picturesque point-of-view of his first teacher, Joseph Silsbee. From his second, more famous master, Louis Sullivan, for whom Wright was working when these "boot-legged" houses were built, the apprentice architect learned the art of geometric simplification, seen so clearly in the taut masses of these houses, especially whenever they are compared to the more ample rounded forms of true Queen Anne residences (No. 63).

8. Walter H. Gale House
1031 Chicago Avenue
Frank Lloyd Wright
1893

Like so many of Wright's early residences, his house of 1893 for druggist Walter Gale (1859-1916) belongs stylistically to the Queen Anne. This is evident in the complexity of its massing, the classical details of its dormer, the Palladian windows in its side gables, and its varied textures of shingles, clapboards, brick and diamond-pane leaded glass. That it is not, however, a conventional Queen Anne house is clear from the geometric purity of its masses. In the latter we may sense the struggle of the young Wright, under the influence of Louis Sullivan's rhetoric, to purify his architecture as Sullivan had done and thus to break from the constraints of the historic styles and invent an original modern style of his own. This is Wright's first completed commission after his break with Adler & Sullivan in mid-1893.

9. Francis J. Woolley House
1030 Superior Street
Frank Lloyd Wright
1893

Certainly not one of Wright's more inspired designs, this house built by Wright in 1893 for attorney Francis J. Woolley, is typical enough of Wright's early low-cost residences. Its high-pitched hip roof, polygonal and rectangular dormers, polygonal bay windows and foundation walls of rough stones laid in irregular courses remind us that Wright's earliest training was in the picturesque manner of Joseph Silsbee. Originally the house was surfaced with narrow clapboards some of which are still exposed on either side of the front steps.

10. Eben E. Roberts House Remodeling
1019 Superior Street
Eben E. Roberts
1911

This was the residence from 1896 to 1932 of architect Eben Roberts, whose firm designed numerous buildings in Oak Park and elsewhere displaying Prairie characteristics. The original structure was extensively remodeled and enlarged by Roberts in 1911. Because its broad surfaces are not subdivided by dark boards and horizontal rows of casement windows, the exterior seems more closely related to the work of modern English architects than to that of Wright and the other leaders of the Prairie School. Why this should be is not entirely clear, especially as the interiors strongly recall the Prairie idiom.

11. Nathan G. Moore House
333 Forest Avenue
Frank Lloyd Wright
1895, 1923

In 1895, with a depression at hand and a growing family, Wright was in no position to argue when his friend and neighbor, Nathan Moore, came to him with the commission for an expensive residence to be designed in the English Tudor style. The building Wright gave Moore with high gables, half-timbering in the upper story, complex medieval chimneys, and diamond-pane casement windows burned at Christmas 1922. Apparently well-satisfied with the original house, Moore returned to Wright for new plans early in 1923.

In reconstructing the house, Wright retained the brick walls of the original house which were still standing. Above them he erected roofs that were even taller and more acutely pointed than those of the original house. Although for Moore's sake Wright may still have pretended to design in the Gothic style, the details of the reconstructed house were conceived mainly in the exotic expressionistic style of Wright's Japanese and California years.

12. Dr. William H. Copeland House Remodeling and Garage
400 Forest Avenue
Frank Lloyd Wright
1908-9

The house was built around 1873 for William H. Harman. Wright's association with Dr. Copeland began in 1908 when he added the garage behind this large late-Italianate house. Wright made provision for an oak tree growing at the southwest corner of the garage. In 1909 Copeland retained Wright again, this time to remodel the house itself. The alterations to the exterior consisted of constructing an entirely new tile roof (removed in the 1950s) above the level of the decorative brickwork on the second story, adding the porches, and replacing the original entrance with doors, frame, sidelights and transom of Wright's own design. Inside the house, Wright thoroughly remodeled the main rooms of the ground floor in conformity with the rigorous dictums of his modern style, and designed the dining room sideboard, table and chairs.

13. Arthur Heurtley House
318 Forest Avenue
Frank Lloyd Wright
1902

Here we encounter one of Wright's truly great residences. It was built in 1902 for banker Arthur Heurtley whose serious dedication to the visual and musical arts must have encouraged Wright to design for his unusual client so splendid a work of art.

Behind the almost continuous band of casement windows of the second floor, and securely sheltered from the elements by the deep soffits of the vast hip roof, are the main rooms of the house. On the left is the dining room, in the middle the living room and on the right a porch that originally was open. At the rear of the house on the same floor are the bedrooms.

Besides its highly compact form, the house is especially distinguished by its variegated brickwork which gives to the lower walls an organic roughness of texture and vibrancy of color that effectively relates the house to its natural surroundings. By continuing the brickwork to the south of the house as a low wall, Wright further emphasized this intended organic embrace of house and grounds.

14. Edward R. Hills House
313 Forest Avenue
Frank Lloyd Wright
1906

In 1906 Wright moved to this site a house that originally had been erected in 1874 by William Gray on the next lot north of it. The commission came from Nathan Moore (No. 11) who wanted the Gray House moved and remodeled by Wright as a residence for his daughter, Mary, and her husband, Edward Hills, an attorney.

When Wright moved the house, he also rotated it ninety degrees so that it faced north. The thorough remodeling that followed removed all traces of the older house which disappeared under a veneer of Wrightian themes: stucco walls subdivided by rough boards stained a dark brown, windows organized into horizontal bands, and roofs whose soffits projected well beyond the walls.

But instead of giving those same roofs the characteristically low profile of his other mature designs, Wright chose for some inexplicable reason to recall in their double slopes and high pitches, the roof types of houses he had designed in the mid-1890s.

Regrettably, the house was severly damaged by a fire while being restored (1976) by Mr. and Mrs. Thomas DeCaro. Reconstruction in 1977 included restoration of features lost in remodeling, including the original arrangement of the second floor "bay" window, which had been separated. The small wooden building in the yard north of the house is a ticket booth from the World's Columbian Exposition of 1893 which has been restored by the DeCaro family. Because of the major restoration effort by the DeCaro family, tour guides often refer to the house as the Hills-DeCaro house.

15. Mrs. Thomas H. Gale House
6 Elizabeth Court
Frank Lloyd Wright
1909

Laura Gale, widow of realtor Thomas Gale (1866-1907) who in 1892 had built two houses on Chicago Avenue (Nos. 6-7) from designs by Wright, built this house for herself and her children in 1909. The house Wright designed for her is by all measures one of the most unusual of his Oak Park years. True, its interior, open from front to rear along the longitudinal axis, had been anticipated in designs of 1903 for houses built in Chicago (Walser) and Buffalo (Barton). But the severe rectilinear geometry of its exterior masses and shapes is nowhere else so strongly emphasized in Wright's residential work either before or after the Gale House. In fact, in his insistent use of abstract geometric shapes for detail and mass in the Gale House, Wright anticipated and may even have inspired modern European architects of the 1920s.

16. Peter A. Beachy House
238 Forest Avenue
Frank Lloyd Wright
1906

No doubt the atypical aspects of this impressive brick and stucco residence erected in 1906 for banker Peter A. Beachy (1859-1945) are to be explained in part by the nature of the commission which was a remodeling. Yet if Wright felt constrained in his planning of this large house by the Gothic cottage that formerly stood on the site, it is not very obvious from the outside except in the way the Beachy House is oriented at right angles to the street in order to utilize a part of its foundations. Perhaps the open gables of the roofs are intended to recall the gables of the Gothic cottage, however, they also resemble the gables in a number of residences built by Wright around the turn of the century. But there are also many details that relate to other buildings by Wright of 1906. For example, the square panes of glass supported by wooden mullions and the three-part window of the ground floor tie this uncommon house firmly to its period of design.

17. Frank W. Thomas House
210 Forest Avenue
Frank Lloyd Wright
1901

This house, built in 1901 by James C. Rogers for his daughter and her husband, Mr. and Mrs. Frank Wright Thomas, is the earliest of Wright's fully mature residences in Oak Park. Thus, it is the first Prairie House in Oak Park. It is also the first house by Wright in Oak Park to have its main rooms raised a full story above grade on a high basement. More important, however, is its distinction as Wright's first all-stucco house in Oak Park, and only the third of its kind by the architect. By changing from wood to stucco for frame houses Wright was able to achieve the kind of precise geometric masses that his rapidly developing modern aesthetic required.

Typical of Wright's houses of 1901-3 is the arched entrance, leaded glass accentuated by bits of white and gold, and the beaded moldings. Unique is the L-shaped plan said to have been suggested by Wright's chief draftsman, Walter Burley Griffin, in order to orient the house toward the more open view to the north and west while blocking from view the high brick wall of the row houses on the south side.

The Thomas House was carefully restored to its original condition (1975) by Mr. and Mrs. Robert Coleman.

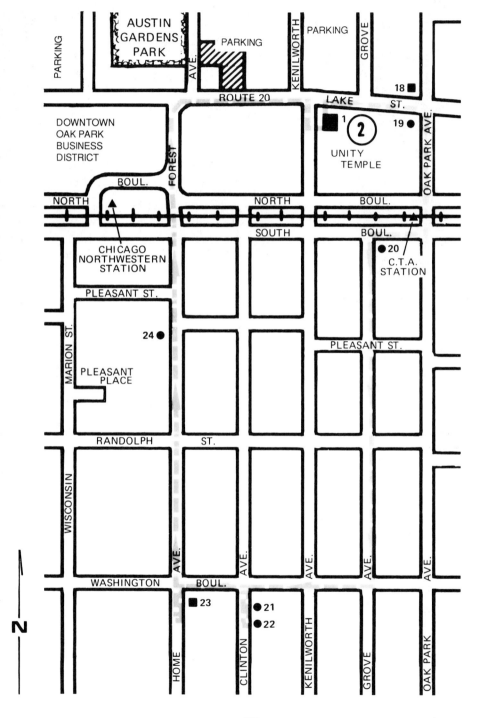

HOME AVENUE — TOUR 2

Approximate Walking Time: one hour, fifteen minutes

1. Unity Temple — 1905-8, *F. L. Wright*	Lake at Kenilworth
18. Horse Show Fountain — 1909, 1969, *R. Bock & F. L. Wright*	Lake at Oak Park
19. Charles B. Scoville Building — 1908, *E. E. Roberts*	137 N. Oak Park
20. George R. Hemingway House — 1914, *J. Van Bergen*	106 S. Grove
21. Frank W. Hall House — 1904-5, *E. E. Roberts*	412 Clinton
22. Charles W. Austin House — 1905, *C. E. White*	420 Clinton
23. George W. Smith House — 1895, 1898, *F. L. Wright*	404 Home
24. John Farson House — 1897-99, *G. W. Maher*	217 Home

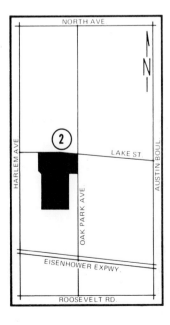

PLEASE . . . with the exception of Unity Temple and the Farson House, the tour buildings described here are not open to the public. Please respect the privacy of the residents and their property and environment. Individuals interested in obtaining further information on specific buildings or guided tour programs may contact the Oak Park Visitors Center (708) 848-1500.

1. Unity Temple
Lake Street at Kenilworth Avenue
Frank Lloyd Wright
1905-8

In its outwardly simple sculptural forms, this three-dimensional monu-
to "the worship of God and the service of man" may seem much less
complicated than it really is. That Wright could thus endow this impressive
composition with so strong a sense of repose, while yet constructing it out of
a series of complexly interlocking rectilinear solids, is a testimony to his
extraordinary gift as a three-dimensional artist. In this respect, Wright far
exceeded the abilities of his teacher, Louis Sullivan, even though it is to
Sullivan's commercial work that the abstract geometric masses of Unity
Temple must ultimately be traced.

Begun in 1906, but not finished until 1908, this religious complex of
church and parish house was constructed throughout of reinforced concrete.
To soften the harshness of the concrete, its pebble aggregate was exposed by
scrubbing and washing the exterior after the forms were removed. The
interior walls were subdivided and accentuated by strips of hardwood, and
their plaster surfaces painted in browns, light greens and yellows.

The church proper is a simple cubic volume of space lighted from above
by a skylight and clerestory windows of art glass. Its balconies, passageways,
and other subsidiary spaces serve, however, to enlarge and expand this central
well of space into a highly complex volume. Wright deliberately placed the
lectern of this liberal church against the entry wall so that the congregation
would depart by walking toward the minister instead of away from him.

18. Horse Show Fountain
Lake Street at Oak Park Avenue
Richard Bock and Frank Lloyd Wright
1909/1969

When originally built in 1909 by the Horse Show Association, this concrete fountain was located on the curb of Lake Street, one hundred feet west of its present position, where it served horses, dogs and people. By 1969 the concrete had so disintegrated that, as a part of the Frank Lloyd Wright Centennial festivities, it was decided to commission a replica and erect it at the entrance to Scoville Green.

Although the fountain is officially the work of Richard Bock, a prominent sculptor who executed much of Wright's architectural sculpture (No. 5) between 1898 and 1913, Wright's name has always been associated with the design. According to Bock, it was Wright who suggested the opening at the center for the drinking fountain. Because in its spatial complexity and involved massing, the fountain resembles Wright's architecture of the period (No. 15), it is likely that Wright was more deeply involved in the design than Bock remembered.

19. Second Scoville Building
137 N. Oak Park Avenue
Eben E. Roberts
1908

Photograph Circa 1910

Roberts' sources for this building, the only major commercial structure ever erected in Oak Park in a Prairie idiom, were assuredly the business buildings of Louis Sullivan and his student, Frank Lloyd Wright. This much is evident in its relatively flat brick walls articulated and subdivided by attenuated brick piers, many of which are returned by arches at the top of the wall, and by the hip roofs that cover the whole of the building.

As originally erected in 1908, the building contained offices and a Masonic hall on its upper floors and shops on the ground floor. Its main entrance was located in the recessed center part of the building facing Oak Park Avenue. The client was Oak Park financier and philanthropist Charles B. Scoville, who earlier had built the first Scoville Apartment and Store Building across the street from this, the second Scoville Building.

The building has been sensitively remodeled by architect John Vinci into shops and offices, and in many places returned to its original form by restoration and reconstruction. Be sure to visit the interior with its impressive staircase, wooden columns and balustrade, and art glass windows. There you can study close up Robert's version of the Prairie, or early modern decorative vocabulary of Sullivan and Wright.

20. George R. Hemingway House
106 S. Grove Avenue
John S. Van Bergen
1914

Although this residence built by Van Bergen in 1914 for realtor George Hemingway (an uncle of Ernest Hemingway) may at first seem visually unrelated to the architect's slightly earlier house for Harry Horder (No. 57) on Fair Oaks Avenue, both houses were in fact built from identical but reversed plans. With its hip roofs, and its second story treated as a frieze, the Hemingway House adheres to the stylistic tradition of Van Bergen's earlier residences while its prototype, the Horder House, with its gable roofs and continuous stucco surfaces breaks new ground. Hemingway, like his counterparts, Joseph Guy (Nos. 42-43) and Flori Blondeel (Nos. 25-27), did not at once find a buyer for this modern house and was forced to rent it until a buyer was finally found in 1924.

21. Frank W. Hall House
412 Clinton Avenue
Eben E. Roberts
1904-5

In this residence by Eben Roberts for lumber dealer Frank Hall, the architect perfected his own version of the Prairie house. This type, which soon would become characteristic of Roberts' residential work, had appeared only a year before in his Magill House (No. 35). As a model of its type the Hall House is of interest in the way its walls are treated, which here consist of two materials, stucco above wood, instead of the single substance, usually stucco, that is typical of Roberts' later houses of this type.

As with other houses of this kind, it is the linear character of its details, the emphasis on rectangular shapes in mass and surface, and the hip roofs with broad eaves that recall Wright's architecture. The full-width porch and general formality of its front are characteristics probably attributable to Maher's work.

22. Charles W. Austin House
420 Clinton Avenue
Charles E. White Jr.
1905

When Charles White designed this house for mathematics teacher, Charles Austin, he was still employed by Frank Lloyd Wright, for whom he had worked since 1903. Although determined from the beginning to evolve a modern style of his own, White did not at once declare his independence from Wright. That much is clear from the number of Wrightian details, such as the base course and wood strips, that White used as part of his design. His dependence on abstract geometry for its massing was, of course, also derived from Wright's work. But by not continuing the bands of wood completely around the second floor of the house, as Wright ordinarily would have done, White shows even in this early work his preference for simple broad masses such as would characterize his work in 1906. (Nos. 28, 53).

22. *Charles W. Austin House*

23. George W. Smith House
404 Home Avenue
Frank Lloyd Wright
(1895) 1898

Although built in 1898 for George Smith, a salesman for Marshall Field & Co., this house was actually designed in 1895 as one of a group of low-cost houses for Charles Roberts that were never built. This fact serves to explain why so retardatory a design as the Smith House has always been firmly documented to the year 1898 — where stylistically it simply does not belong. With its roofs of high pitch and double slope, the house recalls Wright's residence for Harry Goodrich of 1896 (No. 60) which itself may be one of the same low-cost house designs. In place of the shingles used so extensively here, Wright had by 1898 substituted horizontal board-and-batten siding presumably because it was more suitable to his growing interest in linear effects.

24. John Farson House
217 Home Avenue
George W. Maher
1897-99

Compared to Wright's work after 1900 the Farson House may seem perhaps a bit old-fashioned with its formal facade and wide front porch. It was extraordinary however, compared to typical residences of the late 1890's. Its clean lines, flat surfaces of Roman brick, stone and wood, and its simple rectangular window frames, chimneys and porch openings would have been hard to parallel anywhere at that time except in buildings by Sullivan and Wright. It is quite likely that the inspiration for the Farson House was Wright's Winslow House of 1894 in River Forest.

In the evolution of Maher's architecture his Farson House is of signal importance for it was in this design that the architect perfected his own version of Prairie architecture. Before the Farson House, Maher designed mostly picturesque buildings in the organic styles then current. But with the Farson House he entered dramatically into the period of his artistic maturity which henceforth was to be tied directly to the fortunes of those forward-looking early modern architects in the Midwest collectively known as the Prairie School of Architecture.

The romantic-sounding name, "Pleasant Home," given the house by its owner John Farson, and carved into its cornerstone, was in fact concocted by him from the location of the house at the corner of Home and Pleasant Avenues. Farson (1855-1910), a highly successful banker, was a partner in his own firm of Farson, Leach & Co. *Currently the building contains the museum of The Historical Society of Oak Park and River Forest.*

1903

1903

Views of the John Farson House, as it appeared in 1903, from the Philander Barclay Collection.

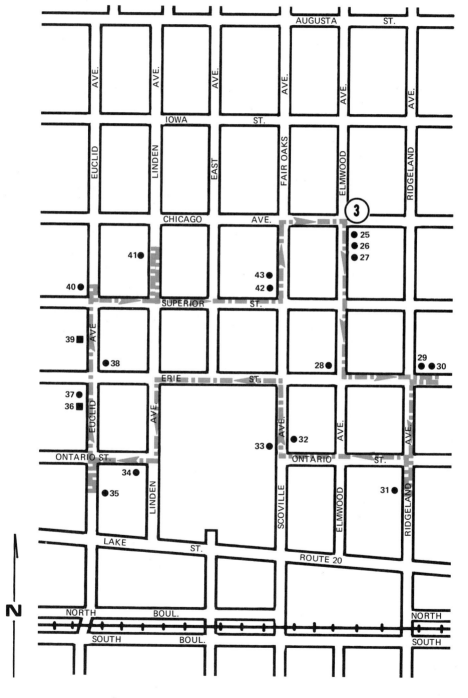

ELMWOOD AVENUE — TOUR 3
Approximate Walking Time: one hour, thirty minutes

25.	Flori Blondeel House — 1914, *J. Van Bergen*	436 N. Elmwood
26.	Flori Blondeel House — 1914, *J. Van Bergen*	432 N. Elmwood
27.	Flori Blondeel House — 1913, *J. Van Bergen*	426 N. Elmwood
28.	Burt L. Wallace House — 1906, *C. E. White*	309 N. Elmwood
29.	Trinity Lutheran Church — 1916, *E. E. Roberts*	300 N. Ridgeland
30.	Trinity Lutheran Chapel — 1909, *E. E. Roberts*	300 N. Ridgeland
31.	William C. Stephens House — 1909-10, *R. C. Spencer*	167 N. Ridgeland
32.	Torrie S. Estabrook House — 1909, *Tallmadge & Watson*	200 N. Scoville
33.	Oak Park-River Forest High School—1905, *R.C. Spencer* 1912, *E.E. Roberts*	Scoville at Ontario
34.	The Linden Apartments — 1915-16, *J. Van Bergen*	175-81 Linden
35.	Henry P. Magill House — 1903, *E. E. Roberts*	164 N. Euclid
36.	George W. Furbeck House — 1897, *F. L. Wright*	223 N. Euclid
37.	Edward W. McCready House — 1907, *R. C. Spencer*	231 N. Euclid
38.	Herman W. Mallen House — 1904-5, *G. W. Maher*	300 N. Euclid
39.	Charles E. Roberts House — 1896, *F. L. Wright*	321 N. Euclid
40.	James Hall Taylor House — 1912, *G. W. Maher*	405 N. Euclid
41.	Gustavus Babson House II — 1912-13, *Tallmadge & Watson*	415 Linden
42.	Joseph S. Guy House — 1915, *Tallmadge & Watson*	407 N. Scoville
43.	Frederick B. Mathis House — 1913, *Tallmadge & Watson*	411 N. Scoville

PLEASE . . . The tour homes described here are private residences and are not open to the public. Please respect the privacy of the residents and their property and environment. Individuals interested in obtaining further information on specific buildings or guided tour programs may contact the Oak Park Visitors Center (708) 848-1500.

Flori Blondeel Houses
25. 436 N. Elmwood Avenue
26. 432 N. Elmwood Avenue
27. 426 N. Elmwood Avenue
John S. Van Bergen
1913-14

Apparently neither Van Bergen nor his client, Flori Blondeel, a florist, had this formal group of Prairie houses in mind when construction began on the house at 426 in the summer of 1913. In fact, at the end of that summer Van Bergen sold the same design, but with the plan reversed, to William Griffith, who erected it at 418 S. Harvey Street in Oak Park. Had Van Bergen known that Blondeel would return for two additional house plans early in 1914, the architect might have made an entirely new design for Griffith and thus have avoided selling identical plans to two different clients in the same community.

Van Bergen's response to Blondeel's commission was to arrange the three houses as a symmetrical composition. The one in the center was derived from the architect's then already much-used square house (Nos. 48, 49, 50, 67, 69), while the one on the left at 436 necessarily became nearly an exact duplicate of the Griffith House on S. Harvey. That the Blondeel commission evolved as it did was certainly fortuitous. It provides the only example in Oak Park of a group of Prairie houses designed as an ensemble, and thus enables the observer to judge for himself the urbanistic benefits of associating in this manner houses of the same style, shape, color, texture and scale.

Although offered for sale when finished, the houses did not at once find buyers and had to be rented for a number of years. Presumably Blondeel's lack of success in disposing of the houses was partly the result of economic disturbances caused by the world war. But it is also highly likely he fell victim to the same changes in architectural taste that were soon to bring down the curtain on the dramatic rise and fall of this first school of modern architecture in America.

28. Burt L. Wallace House
309 N. Elmwood Avenue
Charles E. White Jr.
1906

It was with this house for insurance broker Burt L. Wallace that Charles White finally achieved independence from Wright and evolved a modern style of his own. In this design White has softened the severity of Wright's linear shapes by rounding the plaster eaves and base of the house. He also avoids subdividing the surfaces, or uniting the windows, with the ligaments of wood so much favored by Wright. Perhaps White's sources for these non-Wrightian effects were the stucco dwellings of such modern English architects as Charles Voysey and M. H. Baillie Scott.

29. Trinity Lutheran Church
300 N. Ridgeland Avenue
30. Trinity Lutheran Chapel
300 N. Ridgeland Avenue
Eben E. Roberts
1916, 1909

This Lutheran church on Ridgeland, and the chapel behind it on Erie, are of particular interest, as documents of the changes in taste that were evident just before the first world war. In 1909 Eben Roberts built the chapel in a thoroughly Prairie idiom. The chapel was built with the intention of being used as a parsonage after the church was constructed, but this plan was never put into effect.

The main church, designed and built by Roberts in 1916, evidences an eclectic composition of Prairie and other styles.

30. Trinity Luthern Chapel Circa 1910

The details of the towers, as well as those of the front and side walls of the church, actively employ the geometric shapes of the Prairie idiom. The same is true of window placement and the stained glass. Roberts' design for this building shows both dedication to the ideals and experimentation with the forms of the Prairie School that generally go unnoticed.

Just to the south, at 232 N. Ridgeland, Eben Roberts' 1912 house for local merchant Bert Davis illustrates the Prairie style in its wide overhanging eaves, grouped corner casement windows, elaborate continuous woodwork and pronounced horizontality, emphasized by an asymmetrically placed front porch.

31. William C. Stephens House
167 N. Ridgeland Avenue
Robert C. Spencer Jr.
1909-10

Because of the sharply pointed gable roofs, half-timbering and groups of casement windows, it might seem that Robert Spencer had turned to the Middle Ages for inspiration in designing this charming residence. In fact, the house is a version of Spencer's own mature Prairie idiom. This is apparent in its crisply-articulated geometric masses, and in the way they are subdivided into rectangular units. Even the supposed half-timbering proves when examined carefully to be no more than a rectangular grid of rough boards laid in the stucco. If its owner, William Stephens, an Englishman by birth, fancied himself living in a Tudor cottage, its architect knew that his client was really living in a Prairie house.

32. Torrie S. Estabrook House
200 N. Scoville Avenue
Tallmadge & Watson
1909

Even among the residential designs of Tallmadge & Watson, who seemed to delight in finding new ways of recombining the Prairie vocabulary, this house stands out as being especially atypical. Its cruciform plan, with garage in the basement and double roof on the cross axis, is without parallel in their work. That in 1909 architects should have given so prominent a place to the motorcar in the planning of a house indicates the degree to which the automobile had by then affected American cultural values. Torrie Estabrook owned a wholesale lumber firm in Chicago.

33. Oak Park and River Forest High School   *Erie St. front by E. E. Roberts*

48

Original Ontario Street front by R. C. Spencer
Photograph Circa 1907

Original entrance detail

33. Oak Park and River Forest High School
N. Scoville Avenue at Ontario Street
Robert C. Spencer Jr. and Eben E. Roberts
1905-8, 1912-13

Designed in 1905, and built in 1906, the original building of the present Oak Park and River Forest High School complex faced south, its main entrance opening onto Ontario Street. Although modern additions in the former right-of-way of Ontario Street have all but obliterated that front, we may still gain an idea of its form by examining the eastern side of the original building which overlooks Scoville and runs northward from the modern additions to the polygonal bay. Its architect, Robert Spencer, expressed the spirit of the Prairie School in its overhanging hip roof, horizontally accentuated courses of brick and stone, and the geometric simplification of its walls.

Eben Roberts extended the building northward in 1912 to Erie Street; his additions carried out in the original style housed the physical education, manual training and domestic science departments. The cornerstone and a fountain that formerly were part of the Ontario Avenue front of Spencer's original building, are now built into the wall of the Scoville Street facade. *Rooms preserved in their original form and especially worth examination are the English Room and the Classics Room (Nos. 338 and 339).*

49

34. The Linden Apartments
for Salem E. Munyer
175-81 Linden Avenue, 643-45 Ontario Street
John S. Van Bergen
1915-16

An extremely well-designed apartment building by any standard, this structure also has the distinction of being one of the few buildings of its type to have been designed in a thoroughly Wrightian manner. By 1915 Van Bergen was ready for a commission of this size and scale and he responded admirably to the challenge by producing a notable scheme. For each of the eighteen apartments he provided a glazed and screened front porch and a rear sleeping porch. He also included a wood-burning fireplace in all but the smallest six of them.

The exterior is exceptionally handsome for an apartment building with its horizontally accentuated brick-and-stone walls, united vertically by the projecting porches, massive chimneys, and tall piers that frame the art glass windows of the three entryways. Munyer and his wife, who operated a family business of importing and distributing linen, presumably built the apartments solely as an investment as they did not live there.

35. Henry P. Magill House
164 N. Euclid Avenue
Eben E. Roberts
1903

As the first all-stucco house by Roberts — and the first design by him to utilize the geometric vocabularly of Prairie architecture — this house of 1903 for insurance executive Henry Magill is of considerable significance. Roberts' source of inspiration for the full width front porch, originally unsupported except at the ends, and the formal treatment of the front, was most likely the work of George Maher, especially his Farson House (No. 24), rather than anything by Wright. Roberts was not oblivious to Wright's work, however, as is clear from the Wrightian base course, porch railing and leaded glass. The interesting way the windows of the second and attic stories are linked by a rectangular frame ornamented with linear details is apparently Roberts' own invention.

36. George W. Furbeck House
223 N. Euclid Avenue
Frank Lloyd Wright
1897

Photograph Circa 1900

With this design of early 1897 Wright launched a three-year period of experimentation that would result in the birth of his fully mature modern style of architecture in 1900. In the bargain, George Furbeck got a splendid house for himself and his bride, a house that today is still largely unchanged on the inside. The exterior, however, was altered in 1920 by an enclosed front porch built upon the retaining wall that originally surrounded a smaller open porch, and by a sizeable extension of the original third floor dormer.

Unusual aspects of this experimental design are the stepped limestone foundations, the use of common brick for the walls, and the wooden details of the windows. Looking toward the future is the massive rectangular chimney and the overhanding hip roof. Remaining from Wright's earlier architecture are the octagonal towers, echoed by the octagonal plan of the living room.

37. Edward W. McCready House
231 N. Euclid Avenue
Robert C. Spencer Jr.
1907

In this substantial brick house of 1907 designed for the manager and treasurer of the R. W. McCready Cork Company, we are introduced to Robert Spencer's mature Prairie style. We are reminded of Wright's architecture in the use of mottled Roman brick laid up with the horizontal joints raked out and the verticals flush, casement windows arranged in decorative patterns, and hip roofs of low pitch extending far out beyond the walls. The house nonetheless possesses a distinctive character of its own. This is especially the result of Spencer's propensity for emphasizing the solidity of each mass by avoiding (1) the changes of level in his surfaces, (2) variations of texture, and (3) interconnecting ligaments of stone and brick — the approach that Wright employed so artfully to subdivide his masses and thereby to reduce the scale of his residences. The result, of course, is that Spencer's houses seem more formal and imposing — and thereby also a bit less organic than do Wright's.

The C. A. Sharpe house, across the street at 220 N. Euclid, was designed by Charles White in 1913. This impressive English-style residence has been owned by members of the Dole and Cheney families. Through the generosity of Miss Cheney, possession of this estate has passed to the Park District of Oak Park.

38. Herman W. Mallen House
300 N. Euclid Avenue
George W. Maher
1904-5

Photograph Circa 1910

Although now considerably altered by a veneer of brick laid over its original stucco walls and by the jagged stonework now framing the entrance, this house designed in 1904 by George Maher for furniture manufacturer Herman Mallen is still worth a passing glance. Notice especially the elegant stylized floral patterns of the stained glass and the floral moldings of the balcony over the entrance with its curious, but typical, Maheresque columns.

39. Charles E. Roberts House

Charles E. Roberts Stable

Interior stairway of Charles E. Roberts House

39. Charles E. Roberts House Remodeling and Stable
321 and 317 N. Euclid Avenue
Frank Lloyd Wright
1896

From the outside of this now remodeled Queen Anne house that was designed and built in 1883 for Charles Roberts by the noted Chicago firm of Burnham & Root one would never suspect the riches that lie within. Roberts (1843-1934), president of the Chicago Screw Company, was a remarkable man who, early in the 1890's, set out to nurture and support the young Frank Lloyd Wright in whom he sensed true artistic genius.

In 1896 Wright remodeled the interiors of this house for his patron. The result was one of the most exquisite ensembles of decorative woodwork to survive from of the earliest years of Wright's independent practice.

At the rear of the lot next to Roberts' house on the south is a dwelling, originally built or remodeled by Wright about 1896 as the Roberts' stable, which was moved in 1929 to its present site by Roberts' son-in-law, the architect Charles E. White Jr., who remodeled it into a residence.

40. James Hall Taylor House
405 N. Euclid Avenue
George W. Maher
1912

Maher's large and expensive house for manufacturer James Taylor (now Unity Church of the Daily Word) was the architect's last commission in Oak Park. Built in 1912, it summarizes Maher's strengths and weaknesses. Where in 1912 Wright was about to move into an entirely new phase of architectural design with his expressionistic Midway Gardens of 1913, all that remained for Maher was repetition and synthesis, as this imposing residence testifies. In it we see all of the typical motifs and arrangements that characterized Maher's residences as far back as his Farson House of 1897 (No. 24). Here Maher achieved a perfection of shape, form and plan which he was never to excell.

While at this location, notice the residence at 420 N. Euclid, designed in an English manner by Charles E. White, Jr. The house represents a retreat for White from the Prairie style.

41. Gustavus Babson House II
415 Linden Avenue
Tallmadge & Watson
1912-13

In this large and elaborately detailed Prairie House we can discern certain preferences of its architects, Tallmadge & Watson. They favored open gable roofs, walls composed of several materials, casement and sash windows mixed according to their aesthetic fancy, and complicated wooden details for many of the grouped windows. As these architects were not leaders in the Prairie movement, it is not surprising to find that the entrance seems to have been suggested by the work of George Maher and the gable roofs possibly borrowed from the work of Walter Griffin.

The client, Gustavus Babson, was one of several brothers who operated a mail order business in Chicago. Between them they made a substantial contribution to the fortunes of several early modern architects through commissions for houses and office buildings during the decade from 1905 to 1915. Besides Tallmadge & Watson, the architects who benefited from their patronage were Louis Sullivan and George Elmslie.

42. Joseph S. Guy House

42. Joseph S. Guy House
407 N. Scoville Avenue
Tallmadge & Watson
1915

In their house for Joseph Guy, a contractor who understood the aims of the Prairie architects and built many of their houses in Oak Park, we see Tallmadge & Watson stubbornly carrying on their own version of the Prairie idiom into the summer of 1915. The cubic solidity of this house, with the vertical accents of its substantial piers held in a delicate but firm balance by the horizontal accents of window alignment, foundation wall, stucco band above the brick, and hip roof, demonstrates again that it is wrong to think of Prairie architecture as a style that emphasized only horizontal effects.

43. Frederick B. Mathis House
411 N. Scoville Avenue
Tallmadge & Watson
1913

Built as a speculative venture by contractor Joseph Guy, this house of 1913 by Tallmadge & Watson did not sell until 1915 when it was purchased by Frederick Mathis, a sales manager. With its overhanging gable roofs it resembles the somewhat smaller and less expensive house the architects had designed earlier the same year for William Carroll (No. 51).

Before the stucco gable was added to the porch at the time it was enclosed, its roof floated freely above the porch and visually echoed and affirmed the pointed shapes of window and roof in the house proper.

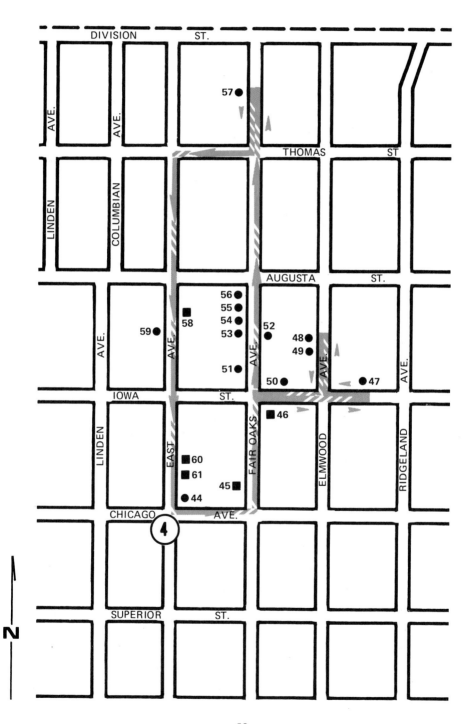

FAIR OAKS AVENUE — TOUR 4

Approximate Walking Time: one hour

44.	Dale Bumstead House — 1909, *Tallmadge & Watson*	504 N. East
45.	Rollin Furbeck House — 1897, *F. L. Wright*	515 Fair Oaks
46.	William G. Fricke House — 1901-02, *F. L. Wright*	540 Fair Oaks
47.	Gustavus Babson House I — 1906, *Tallmadge & Watson*	412 Iowa
48.	Albert H. Manson House — 1911-12, *J. Van Bergen*	619 N. Elmwood
49.	Mrs. R. D. Manson House — 1911-12, *J. Van Bergen*	615 N. Elmwood
50.	Mrs. Charles S. Yerkes House — 1912-13, *J. Van Bergen*	450 Iowa
51.	William V. Carroll House — 1913, *Tallmadge & Watson*	611 Fair Oaks
52.	Frank H. Lauder House — 1907, *Tallmadge & Watson*	626 Fair Oaks
53.	Charles W. Helder House — 1906, *C. E. White*	629 Fair Oaks
54.	Charles Schwerin House — 1908, *E. E. Roberts*	639 Fair Oaks
55.	Vernon S. Watson House — 1904, *V. S. Watson*	643 Fair Oaks
56.	Otto McFeely House — 1905, *V. S. Watson*	645 Fair Oaks
57.	Harry G. Horder House — 1914, *J. Van Bergen*	823 Fair Oaks
58.	William E. Martin House — 1903, *F. L. Wright*	636 N. East
59.	Barrett Andrews House — 1906, *Tallmadge & Watson*	623 N. East
60.	Harry C. Goodrich House — 1895-96, *F. L. Wright*	534 N. East
61.	Edwin H. Cheney House — 1903-04, *F. L. Wright*	520 N. East

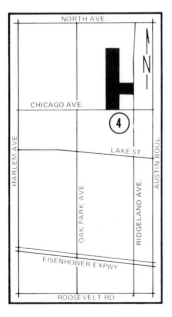

PLEASE . . . The tour homes described here are private residences and are not open to the public. Please respect the privacy of the residents and their property and environment. Individuals interested in obtaining further information on specific buildings or guided tour programs may contact the Oak Park Visitors Center (708) 848-1500.

44. Dale Bumstead House
504 N. East Avenue
Tallmadge & Watson
1909

This residence for Dale Bumstead is one of a group of stucco and brick houses designed by Tallmadge & Watson around 1910 that incorporate narrow piers as a major ingredient in their wall surfaces. Of the others, which include one in Oak Park (No. 74), the Bumstead House is certainly the most substantial looking. Its surfaces are bound firmly together by an interlocking system of sharp-edged piers, fascias, sills, and windows, all echoing and reinforcing the rigid rectilinearity of plan and mass. So monumental a design, without strong parallels in the work of other Prairie architects, might well have served Tallmadge & Watson as the model for a Prairie style of their own. But with their preference for variety and indifference to stylistic continuity, the architects never exploited the implications of the Bumstead House.

45. Rollin Furbeck House
515 Fair Oaks Avenue
Frank Lloyd Wright
1897

Wright designed this house for Rollin Furbeck about six months after the one that he built on Euclid Avenue for Rollin's brother George (No. 36). Apparently the houses were wedding presents to the brothers (who were both married in 1897) from their stockbroker father, Warren. Although the elder Furbeck did not himself live in a Wright-designed house, he may have selected the architect of his sons' houses. If he did, it may partly explain why neither brother lived in his new house very long. Rollin selling in November, 1898, and George in September, 1899.

But whatever the brothers really thought about their dwellings, each house is of considerable interest to the historian. It was with these designs that Wright launched a three-year period of experimentation that by 1900 had led him to his own mature style of modern architecture. Premonitions of that style appear in the Rollin Furbeck House in its solid rectangular masses, its horizontally accentuated stucco band between brick wall and roof, and in its hip roof of low pitch. Aspects of the house eventually abandoned by Wright are the narrow three-story center section, including its octagonal columns, and the complex brickwork of base course, porch piers and walls.

46. William G. Fricke House
540 Fair Oaks Avenue
Frank Lloyd Wright
1901-2

Like the house Wright designed earlier in 1901 for Frank Thomas on Forest Avenue (No. 17), this all-stucco house for William Fricke is a mixture of elements — some of which were to sustain the architect throughout the remainder of his Oak Park years, with others that were soon to be discarded. Notable among the latter is the massive square tower that rises skyward out of the otherwise horizontally accentuated walls and roofs of the Iowa Street side. Also soon to disappear from Wright's style was his use of rectangular columns ornamented with linear details in dark wood that appear in many of the windows, and the beaded frames surrounding a number of them.

That Wright was a consummate artist when dealing with three-dimensional shapes, is perhaps better revealed in this house than in any other in Oak Park. Its complex masses, and the exterior spaces they generate and define, are here interlocked in such an intricate embrace, that the idea of "wall" in the traditional sense, is completely undone.

As originally built, there was an open pavilion on the south side (where the relatively new brick residence now stands). It was connected to the house between the two groups of windows on the south side by a covered passageway.

47. Gustavus Babson House I
412 Iowa Street
Tallmadge & Watson
1906

Gustavus Babson was not yet very prosperous when he had the newly-founded firm of Tallmadge & Watson build this modest house for his family. In order to reduce costs in 1906, his architects experimented with panels "of pebbled roofing felt which resembles plaster" for the walls of the second floor and used a relatively cheap wood for trimming the interiors. That these young architects had been inspired by Wright's work when designing this house seems clear from its straight lines, rectangular shapes, continuous base course, band of casement windows in the second floor, and overhanging hip roof.

48. Albert H. Manson House
619 N. Elmwood Avenue
49. Mrs. R. D. Manson House
615 N. Elmwood Avenue
John S. Van Bergen
1911-12

Built as rental houses by Elizabeth and her son Albert Manson, these are the earliest known independent designs by John Van Bergen. They were begun only a few months after the young architect passed the Illinois architectural licensing examination and entered into private practice.

In plan and general configuration the two houses are based on Wright's fireproof house project of 1907. Van Bergen sought, however, to vary their forms and details so that each has its own personality. Even so, in the house for Albert Manson, Van Bergen found it convenient to rely heavily on his master's project. There he repeated almost line for line the base course, planter surmounted by two rows of casement windows, massive corner piers, and overhanging slab roof of the fireproof house project.

Both houses also have ground floor plans based on Wright's project. At the center of each there is a large chimney which acts as the pivot of a continuously open L-shaped interior space that runs across the front and down the left side of each house and serves as the combined living and dining rooms. In the remaining corner on the right side at the rear is the kitchen which is treated as a separate room. Between it and the living room are the entry hall and staircase.

50. Mrs. Charles S. Yerkes House
450 Iowa Street
John S. Van Bergen
1912-13

No doubt Van Bergen chose clapboards for the lower walls of this house in a search for variety while working within the limitations imposed by the residential type introduced by Wright in his fireproof house project of 1907. That this small house was obviously built on a tight budget probably explains why Van Bergen did not use the aesthetically more desirable but also more expensive horizontal board-and-batten siding favored by Wright. Except for enclosing the porch, it does not appear that the house has been altered since Van Bergen built it in 1912 for the widow of Charles Yerkes.

51. William V. Carroll House
611 Fair Oaks Avenue
Tallmadge & Watson
1913

In using corner piers that rise unobstructed to the overhanging gable roof of this house, Tallmadge & Watson may have been inspired to some degree by the architecture of Wright's former chief draftsman, Walter Burley Griffin. The plan, however, with the main living space completely open from front to rear at the center of the house except for a partial divider, was most likely their own idea.

At the time the architects built this residence for William Carroll, a dispatcher for the New York Central Railroad, the window sash was painted a light color, perhaps white, and the window frames and other trim were stained a dark color. On the south side, the two porches, one above the other, which are now permanently enclosed, were then open.

52. Frank H. Lauder House
626 Fair Oaks Avenue
Tallmadge & Watson
1907

Full credit for this delightful variation on the typical small and inexpensive Prairie house must go to the architects Tallmadge & Watson, who repeated the type in several variations on Chicago's north shore. The way the windows of the second floor become acutely-pointed gables as they rise into the roof is especially charming. Equally attractive is the way the windows are framed by broad flat boards, and every third course of shingles is reduced in width to produce a vivacious surface texture. An old photograph shows that the original color scheme was more alive than it is today: the sash was painted a light color, the shingles stained a medium tone, and the wide flat trim, which today hardly stands out at all from the shingles, stained a dark color.

53. Charles W. Helder House
629 Fair Oaks Avenue
Charles E. White Jr.
1906

In giving greater emphasis to straight lines, right angles, and flat stucco surfaces, White comes closer in this house to the work of Wright and other Prairie architects than he does in his exactly contemporary Wallace House (No. 28), where his sources seem more decidedly English. Although in his design of the porch, bay window in the second floor, and hip roofs White also pays homage to Wright, the peculiar way he combined them is the architect's own. By implying symmetry while actually designing an unbalanced front, White introduced an unresolved tension into this otherwise peaceful dwelling. This has the effect, if that was his aim, of avoiding the monotony of an entirely balanced front.

54. Charles Schwerin House
639 Fair Oaks Avenue
Eben E. Roberts
1908

Of all Roberts' stucco houses in Oak Park, this one designed in 1908 for Charles Schwerin is perhaps the most typical. Only in the broad curve of its attic dormer does it vary from the norm. Otherwise, the house is a model of Roberts' mature Prairie style in its monumental full-width front porch, whose roof is supported only at the ends by stout piers, and in its grouped casement windows, decorative details, broad stucco masses, and symmetrical front.

55. Vernon S. Watson House
643 Fair Oaks Avenue
Vernon S. Watson
1904

What we learn from this diminutive dwelling — designed in the Prairie idiom by architect Vernon Watson well over a year before the partnership of Tallmadge & Watson was founded — is that it was Watson who was responsible for the Prairie designs of the firm.

When Watson designed the house as his residence early in 1904, while he was still working for Daniel Burnham, he had little money to spend on its construction and was forced to make it so small that additions were later required. But as the alterations were made by the architect-owner, they were so skillfully done as to be almost undetectable. At the rear, which may be viewed from the alley, Watson added a small bay of triangular shape, in plan, to the kitchen and at the front he enlarged the living room with a polygonal addition.

Originally the board-and-batten siding was stained a soft brown and the clapboards, a moss-green. The stucco was tinted a light yellow ochre.

56. Otto McFeely House

70

56. Otto H. McFeely House
645 Fair Oaks Avenue
Vernon Watson
1905

Given its severe rectangular mass, thin moldings, and sharply geometric roof shapes, the McFeely House is unusual in Watson's work. Perhaps its distinctive attributes resulted from the type of construction used for its outside walls which are stucco. The additions at the rear were made by Watson for a subsequent owner. Otto McFeely, who wrote for the *Chicago Evening Post* when the house was built, later became editor of *Oak Leaves*, the most prominent newspaper in Oak Park.

57. Harry G. Horder House
823 Fair Oaks Avenue
John S. Van Bergen
1914

Especially because of its projecting gable roofs, Van Bergen's house of 1914 for stationery-business owner, Harry Horder, provides a refreshing change from the sameness of the small cube-like houses the architect designed before the first world war. Its plan, with the living and dining rooms occupying one large undifferentiated space running across the front of the house, is also an unusual variation of Van Bergen's early interior arrangements.

Originally the exterior wood was stained brown and the stucco tinted a cream color. One entered, as now, on the south side but from a porch protected by a low wall on the left containing a flower box and at the rear by a built-in seat. A nearly identical entry porch still exists at the George Hemingway House, also by Van Bergen, on South Grove Avenue (No. 20).

58. William E. Martin House
636 N. East Avenue
Frank Lloyd Wright
1903

An even more indecisive design than the Fricke House of 1901-2 (No. 46) is Wright's 1903 residence for William Martin. Once again the architect could not seem to make up his mind whether he wanted to build horizontally or vertically. This observation is not intended to denigrate the design, however, for the generally vertical pile-up of complexly interlocked rectangular masses and shapes makes a striking composition. It must not, however, have entirely satisfied Wright for after the Martin House, the architect kept his large houses low and let them spread out horizontally.

But whatever Wright may personally have thought of the result, this handsome residence caught the eye of Martin's brother Darwin, principal in the Larkin Company of Buffalo, New York, during a visit in 1903. The result was a series of six houses and an office building in Buffalo for Darwin Martin, his associates in the Larkin Company, and a relative. For William Martin, president of the Martin & Martin Stove Polish Company in Chicago, Wright would also later build a factory.

At one time there were extensive formal gardens on the south side of the house between the street and the alley in the area now occupied by a modern brick house. A long pergola connected the house with the gardens.

59. Barrett Andrews House
623 N. East Avenue
Tallmadge & Watson
1906

Although built by the then newly-organized firm of Tallmadge & Watson, this residence must have been entirely Watson's own. It was Otto McFeely, whose house Watson had built on Fair Oaks Avenue in 1905 (No. 56), who brought the architects and Barrett Andrews together.

As Watson was obviously experimenting at that time with various combinations of Prairie mannerisms picked up from Wright and Maher, it is not surprising that this house should look so unlike either Watson's own house (No. 55) or McFeely's. The architect's extensive use of narrow clapboards, originally stained a dark brown, for the walls give the dwelling a rustic quality that would be hard to parallel except in summer cottages by the Prairie architects. However, the formality of the symmetrical front seems out of character with its roughness of finish and organic color scheme.

60. Harry C. Goodrich House
534 N. East Avenue
Frank Lloyd Wright
(1895) 1896

Like Wright's Smith House of 1898 (No. 23), the dwelling he built in 1896 for inventor Harry Goodrich apparently goes back to a group of low-cost houses Wright designed but did not build in 1895 for his early patron Charles Roberts. Thus, although this house was definitely built in the summer of 1896, it is probably speaking to us largely in Wright's vocabulary of 1895. If this speculation is correct, then we have a reasonable explanation for the wide visual gulf separating the Goodrich House from Wright's Furbeck Houses (Nos. 36, 45) of early 1897.

But even in this seemingly commonplace work there are premonitions of the future. Although he built the house on a basement partly above grade, Wright sought to disguise that fact in the Goodrich House by carrying its narrow clapboards down to a sloping wooden base course at grade level. In the wall elevations there is also a suggestion of his mature manner: base course, wall carried to a stringcourse under the windows of the second floor, horizontal band linking those windows, overhanging roof.

Even in the high roof of double pitch there is a hint of Wright's later ubiquitous hip roofs. If the lower part of that roof is mentally carried up to where its sides would intersect, the result is a hip roof of low pitch.

61. Edwin H. Cheney House
520 N. East Avenue
Frank Lloyd Wright
1903-4

Like the Heurtley House (No. 13), Wright's residence for electrical engineer Edwin Cheney is another superb brick house with the living and sleeping rooms all on one floor under a single broad hip roof. Here, however, there is a less monumental and more intimate quality to the house partly because it is not raised a full story off the ground and partly because of the way its windows are nestled in so protected a fashion between the wide eaves of the roof and the substantial stone sill that girdles the house. This recessive quality must have been even more pronounced when the house was surrounded by its ten-foot-high garden walls.

Its living rooms, which take up the entire front of the house and open onto the walled terrace at the center, are beautifully trimmed in fir. Together they form a single longitudinal space under a continuous ceiling carried up in the form of a hip roof, the whole subdivided into dining room, living room, and library by wooden posts and cabinets.

As is well known, it was this commission that precipitated the celebrated love affair between Wright and Mrs. Cheney, the climax of which occurred in 1909 when Wright abandoned his architectural practice and left with Mrs. Cheney for a year in Europe. The final chapter, however, was not written until 1914 when Mrs. Cheney and her children were murdered at Taliesin by an insane servant.

Across the street, the Frank V. Skiff House (525 N. East Avenue) and Frank P. Ross House (531 N. East Avenue), completed in 1909, were designed by Howard Van Doren Shaw, a prominent architect known nationally for his historical architectural designs. Mr. Ross was the founder of the Jewel Tea Company.

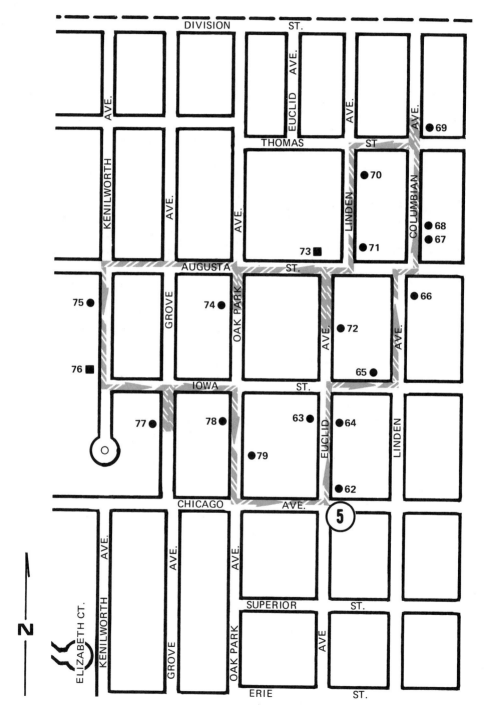

AUGUSTA STREET — TOUR 5

Approximate Walking Time: one hour, twenty minutes

62.	Arthur Basse House — 1920, *Tallmadge & Watson*	506 N. Euclid
63.	Sampson Rogers House — 1896, *E. E. Roberts*	537 N. Euclid
64.	Charles R. Erwin House — 1905, *G. W. Maher*	530 N. Euclid
65.	James Fletcher Skinner House — 1908-9, *C. E. White*	605 Linden
66.	Henry D. Golbeck House — 1914-15, *Tallmadge & Watson*	636 Linden
67.	Robert N. Erskine House — 1913-14, *J. Van Bergen*	714 Columbian
68.	Philip Greiss House — 1914, *J. Van Bergen*	716 Columbian
69.	William H. Watt House — 1913, *J. Van Bergen*	806 Columbian
70.	John W. Bingham House — 1915, *Tallmadge & Watson*	730 Linden
71.	Henry R. Hamilton House — 1914, *J. Van Bergen*	714 Linden
72.	Ashley C. Smith House — 1908, *Tallmadge & Watson*	630 N. Euclid
73.	Harry S. Adams House — 1913-14, *F. L. Wright*	710 Augusta
74.	Harold H. Rockwell House — 1910, *Tallmadge & Watson*	629 N. Oak Park
75.	Whitney T. Lovell House — 1906-7, *Tallmadge & Watson*	635 N. Kenilworth
76.	Oscar B. Balch House — 1911, *F. L. Wright*	611 N. Kenilworth
77.	Louis H. Brink House — 1909, *E. E. Roberts*	533 N. Grove
78.	Albert J. Elliott House — 1908-9, *E. E. Roberts*	539 N. Oak Park
79.	Dr. Charles E. Cessna House — 1905, *E. E. Roberts*	524 N. Oak Park

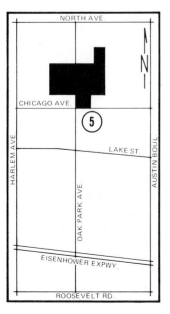

PLEASE . . . The tour homes described here are private residences and are not open to the public. Please respect the privacy of the residents and their property and environment. Individuals interested in obtaining further information on specific buildings or guided tour programs may contact the Oak Park Visitors Center (708) 848-1500.

63. Sampson Rogers House

62. Arthur A. Basse House
506 N. Euclid Avenue
Tallmadge & Watson
1920

63. Sampson Rogers House
537 N. Euclid Avenue
Eben E. Roberts
1896

Although at opposite ends of the block, and by different architects, these houses together occupy pivotal positions in the saga of the Prairie School in Oak Park. The one at 537 for Sampson Rogers, built in 1896 by Eben Roberts, is an excellent example of the suburban Queen Anne style that preceded Prairie architecture. The other at 506, designed in 1920 by Tallmadge & Watson, is a fine example of the scholarly historicism that gradually overwhelmed and replaced both the Queen Anne, and in its turn, the Prairie idiom.

In these two residences we thus have at once the beginning and the end of Prairie architecture, for it was partly out of the inventive historicism of the Queen Anne that the Prairie School was born, and it was in response to the triumphant progress of scholarly historicism that the Prairie School withered and died.

Roberts' house for Sampson Rogers of Bolles and Rogers, dealers in hides and wool, is an involved and picturesque composition made up of complexly interwoven masses and volumes that do not in themselves refer to any easily identifiable historic prototype. Many of the details such as the columns and railing of the porch are derived from eighteenth-century American classicism.

After this house, Roberts' designs gradually became more abstract geometrically and then began to acquire Prairie characteristics.

By contrast, Tallmadge & Watson who had designed almost all of their pre-world war residences in the Prairie manner, discovered that their post-war clients insisted on historic designs of the most scholarly sort. Such was surely the case when in 1920 attorney Arthur Basse commissioned Tallmadge & Watson to design this fine Georgian Revival residence at 506 N. Euclid Avenue.

64. Charles R. Erwin House
530 N. Euclid Avenue
George W. Maher
1905

Of Maher's impressive houses that follow in the tradition of his Farson House (No. 24), this is without doubt the most irregular. Not only is its monumental entry pavilion off center but also its windows do not fall into any discernible pattern.

Unfortunately, the house has been much altered by the various owners who succeeded Maher's client, Charles Erwin, president of a world-wide advertising agency. Gone are the magnificent iron fences whose shape followed the form of the entryway. Replacing the exquisite art glass that originally graced the front and side doors, discarded when it became too expensive to repair, are panels of ornamental etched glass designed by the present owner (1975).

65. James Fletcher Skinner House
605 Linden Avenue
Charles E. White Jr.
1908-9

One reason why this house for J. Fletcher Skinner, of Sears Roebuck & Co., seems so unlike Charles White's earlier stucco houses (Nos. 28, 53) is its large size and its complex but not especially well-unified masses. In 1908, when Skinner went to White with the commission for what was to be one of the most expensive homes in Oak Park up to that time, White apparently was simply unprepared to design on so grand a scale. Although White was never one to miss the opportunity for publicizing his work, and he did illustrate the Skinner House in numerous books and journals, he must not have been entirely pleased with the result for he never again built another house quite like it.

66. *Henry D. Golbeck House*

80

66. Henry D. Golbeck House
636 Linden Avenue
Tallmadge & Watson
1914-15

Built for furniture manufacturer Henry Golbeck, this house is a good example of a mature Prairie design by Tallmadge & Watson just before they abandoned modern architecture. Typical of their work at that time was a propensity for walls of varied and contrasted materials: cement base course, brick carried to the sills of the second story windows, plaster for the frieze, and open gables decorated with wooden details and casement windows. The gable roofs, open porch, and entrance from the porch are also typical.

67. Robert N. Erskine House
714 Columbian Avenue
John S. Van Bergen
1913-14

For a residence so obviously based on Wright's fireproof house project of 1907, it is strange that Van Bergen should have provided this house of 1913 for attorney Robert Erskine with so unusual a plan. Instead of locating the entry on the side of the house opposite the porch, as Van Bergen did in all of his other houses of this type, including the Greiss next door (No. 68), here the house is entered from the porch. But as the staircase remained on the opposite side of the house, Van Bergen found it necessary to connect the entry and stairs by a narrow hallway that completely destroys the spatial continuity of the plan. Presumably this unsatisfactory arrangement was somehow the result of the client's wishes.

68. Philip Greiss House
716 Columbian Avenue
John S. Van Bergen
1914

Van Bergen's house of 1914 for Philip Greiss was the last of his houses in Oak Park to be based on Wright's fireproof house project of 1907, and without doubt, the most severely cubistic of them. Its closest rival is Van Bergen's early house for Albert Manson (No. 48), which also has flat rather than hip roofs. But the masses of the Greiss House seem more emphatically solid because of the way their surfaces are continued without the changes in level that somewhat soften the geometric austerity of the Manson House.

69. William H. Watt House

69. William H. Watt House
806 Columbian Avenue
John S. Van Bergen
1913

Among Van Bergen's many houses of this type, the one he built in 1913 for William Watt seems the most perfect and is also the one that has come down to us with the fewest alterations. That auditor William Watt was satisfied with his house is certain, for when he moved to Lombard after the first world war he engaged Van Bergen to design another house for him.

70. John W. Bingham House
730 Linden Avenue
Tallmadge & Watson
1915

This and the house on N. Scoville for Joseph Guy (No. 42) were the last Prairie houses Tallmadge & Watson ever built in Oak Park. One might argue, of course, that this house, constructed in the summer of 1915 for freight agent John Bingham, is really not a Prairie house at all because of its half-timbering. But, as with other houses of its type (Nos. 31, 74), the medieval effect is quite ephemeral and vanishes whenever the half-timbering is understood for what it really is: an abstract rectilinear subdivision of selected surfaces of the house. In this sense, the design is without dependence on historic prototypes and thus is modern.

71. Henry R. Hamilton House
714 Linden Avenue
John S. Van Bergen
1914

Even if shorn of its third story, which was added by architects Tallmadge & Watson in 1924, this would be an unusual house of its type by Van Bergen. To begin with, the two-story porch on its south side is unique in the architect's early work. Then there is the window glass which is atypical in being held by metal instead of wooden mullions. Finally, there is the uncommonly small scale of its details: groups of five windows in place of the four ordinarily used, relatively small panes of glass in the windows, and especially narrow strips of wood for surface articulation. The owner, Henry Hamilton (1861-1940), who was in the paint business, served as president of the Village of Oak Park from 1907 to 1909.

The success of the Tarzan stories enabled Edgar Rice Burroughs to buy the nearby house at 700 North Linden. This was the popular author's last Oak Park residence, before moving to California to assist in filming of the first Tarzan movies.

72. Ashley C. Smith House
630 N. Euclid Avenue
Tallmadge & Watson
1908

Related to a group of similar but generally formal houses built by Tallmadge & Watson between 1907 to 1909 in Chicago's north shore suburbs, this house of 1908 differs from the others primarily in its asymmetrical composition. The one element that all of these houses share in common is the highly decorated window in the attic, a motif presumably suggested by similar arrangements in residences by George Maher. It is a bit strange that, of all the Prairie architects, these talented young men never seemed able to come up with a Prairie manner of their own, but instead continued to rely on other architects for visual ideas which, as here, they skillfully blended together. Unfortunately investment banker Ashley Smith (1837-1910) hardly had time to enjoy his new house before he passed away in April 1910.

Note that the Smith House and the three nearby located in the middle of the 600 block of North Euclid illustrate several architectural styles. The house for F. G. Baker at 625 N. Euclid, built in 1887 by W. J. Van Keuren, is an example of the Queen Anne style. There is a Colonial Revival residence at 637 N. Euclid, which was built for W. W. Page in 1894. In 1904 Eben Roberts built an elaborate Medieval Revival design for contractor H. C. Todd at 620 N. Euclid.

73. Harry S. Adams House
710 Augusta Street
Frank Lloyd Wright
1913-14

As the last of Wright's Oak Park houses, built at the very moment he was erecting the expressionistic Midway Gardens with which he launched his Japanese and California periods, this residence of 1913 for Harry Adams is of far more than passing interest. With it Wright provided a superb summation of his first modern style and, at the same time, ended his Prairie or Oak Park period. Even though Wright would continue in later designs to recall elements of his Oak Park manner, he would not again design so typical a Prairie house.

Its longitudinal plan with, from left to right, porte cochere, porch, living room, hall and dining room, allowed Wright to display all of the horizontal forms which he had evolved and exploited so magnificently during his Oak Park years: concrete base course, terrace wall on the left responding to the flower box under the three-part dining room window on the right, lower hip roof, continuous string course, casement windows, and main hip roof with its wide eaves. Here there is also Wright's typically indirect approach to the entrance, his ubiquitous but elegantly-designed concrete flower pot on one side of the steps, and in the front door and elsewhere, his exquisite stained glass. Above it all hovers the aesthetic and symbolic mass of the great rectangular chimney.

74. Harold H. Rockwell House
629 N. Oak Park Avenue
Tallmadge & Watson
1910

Harold Rockwell was clearly not a pretentious man for when he built this relatively inexpensive residence on a narrow fifty-foot lot in 1910 he was already an assistant secretary of Chicago's Northern Trust Company and a trustee of the Village of Oak Park. The dwelling that his architects, Tallmadge & Watson, gave him was one of a group of solid-looking all-stucco houses which included the Matthews (No. 3) and Bumstead (No. 44) Houses, both designed in 1909. Evidentally this substantial residence with its strong base course, impressive piers, and massive stucco walls gave its banker-owner a sense of security that suited him for he continued to live here until his death in 1939 by which time he had become vice-president and secretary of the Northern Trust, in Chicago.

75. Whitney T. Lovell House
635 N. Kenilworth Avenue
Tallmadge & Watson
1906-7

Photograph from Modern American Homes
(c1912) (Plate 28) by Hermann von Holst*

Like the McFeely House of 1905 (No. 56), this unusual residence must be classified as an experimental design representing a line of aesthetic development that Tallmadge & Watson apparently did not pursue further. But even though the architects never again designed anything else like it, the house remains for us an intriguing mixture of historic and Prairie details. Among the former is the gambrel roof and shingled walls, and the stout columns that formerly carried the second story above a deep porch where the entrance and four-part casement window are now situated. The Prairie details include the decorative wooden framework of the two-story bay on the right, and the geometric subdivisions of the windows.

With the assistance of the Oak Park Landmarks Commission, Modern American Homes was reprinted by Dover Publications in 1982 under the title, Country and Suburban Homes of the Prairie School Period. This book features many houses in the Oak Park-River Forest area, and provides an excellent photographic overview of the influence of Prairie School architecture throughout the United States. Architect von Holst assumed Wright's practice when Wright left Oak Park in 1909.

76. Oscar B. Balch House
611 N. Kenilworth Avenue
Frank Lloyd Wright
1911

Wright's house for interior decorator Oscar Balch, carried out during the summer of 1911, was one of his first commissions after returning from Europe. In its stark geometry of form, and in the horizontal linearity of its flat roofs, the house appears to continue the line of development begun by Wright in his house of 1909 for Mrs. Gale on Elizabeth Court (No. 15). But if the Balch House does descend from that forward-looking design, it is strange that in planning the house Wright should have found it necessary to resurrect his very early three-part arrangement for the living spaces. The resulting spatial organization, with music room, living room opening onto a terrace, and dining room arranged across the front of the house from left to right, led him to design an equally formal and even somewhat mechanical street elevation that lacks the vigor and finesse of some of Wright's other designs.

Note the C. E. Hemingway house across the street at 600 N. Kenilworth. This was the boyhood home of author Ernest Hemingway, winner of Nobel and Pulitzer prizes. The house was designed for Dr. Hemingway and his artistic wife in 1906 by Henry G. Fiddelke. Ernest Hemingway's birth place, a few blocks away, is marked with a plaque at 339 N. Oak Park Avenue.

77. Louis H. Brink House
533 N. Grove Avenue
Eben E. Roberts
1909

Another large stucco house in the tradition of Roberts' Magill House of 1903 (No. 35), this design of 1909 is distinguished from the others by its unusual curvilinear dormers. Typical of its type are the overhanging hip roof of moderate pitch, casement and sash windows mixed, full-width porch, and distinctive linear ornament. Its first owner, Louis Brink (1865-1931), operated Brink & Sons, one of Chicago's oldest produce and commission houses.

78. Albert J. Elliott House

90

78. Albert J. Elliott House
539 N. Oak Park Avenue
Eben E. Roberts
1908-9

Designed in 1909 and built in 1910 for furrier Albert J. Elliott, this fine house by Eben Roberts exhibits a split personality. Its half-timbered gables seem to recall medieval architecture, even though otherwise the house is clearly in Roberts' Prairie manner. In fact, if these gables are eliminated mentally, the rectangular geometry of its masses, shapes, and details bring the Prairie character sharply into focus. Given so high a degree of modernism, we must suppose the half-timbered gables were included to satisfy the client.

79. Dr. Charles E. Cessna House
524 N. Oak Park Avenue
Eben E. Roberts
1905

Roberts' house of 1905 for Dr. Charles Cessna, a physician, is one of his most elaborately detailed residences of the Magill type (No. 35). In it, Roberts' manner of assembling forms and details derived from a variety of sources is more pronounced than in almost any other residence by him. Thus, in addition to its Prairie characteristics, the house has a rich surface texture of brick, stucco, and wood that even includes a very non-Wrightian tile roof. The sinuous lines of its exquisite floral art glass, and the curvilinear brackets of porch and bay windows, introduce shapes that also contribute to the eclecticism of the design by vying for attention with the straight lines that otherwise predominate.

THE ARCHITECTS

George Washington Maher
b. December 25, 1864   Mill Creek, W. Va.
d. September 12, 1926   Douglas, Michigan

Educated in the public schools of New Albany, Indiana, George Maher began his architectural education in 1878 as an apprentice to the Chicago firm of Bauer & Hill and finished his training in the office of Joseph L. Silsbee. In December 1888 he entered a partnership with Charles Corwin which lasted until June 1893 when Maher went to Europe for a year of study and sketching. Following his return from Europe, he married Elizabeth Brooks on October 25, 1894. Maher resumed architectural practice the same year, but practiced alone until 1921 when he was joined by his son, Philip.

Robert Closson Spencer, Jr.

b. April 13, 1864   Milwaukee, Wisconsin
d. September 9, 1953   Tucson, Arizona

A graduate of the University of Wisconsin in Mechanical Engineering in 1886, Spencer went on to study architecture from 1880-90 at M.I.T. While in the East he married Ernestine Elliott of Bath, Me., on Nov. 28, 1889. After several years of additional study in Europe as holder of the Rotch Traveling Fellowship, he worked for Shepley, Rutan and Coolidge, first in Boston and then in Chicago.

In 1894 he began an independent practice in Chicago which lasted until 1905 when he took Horace Powers as partner. Spencer & Powers continued until 1923 and after that Spencer practiced alone until 1928 when he joined the architecture faculty at Oklahoma A. and M. College. From 1930 to 1934 he taught at the University of Florida, then painted murals for the Federal Government in Florida, finally retiring to Arizona in 1938.

He also invented a number of window opening devices for casement windows and in 1906 founded the Chicago Casement Hardware Co. to manufacture and distribute them.

Eben Ezra Roberts

b.   1866   Boston, Massachusetts
d. August 4, 1943   Muskegon, Michigan

Educated in the public schools of Boston, Massachusetts, and trained by his father in mechanical and freehand drawing. Eben E. Roberts later studied at the Tilton Academy in New Hampshire. Between 1889 and 1893 Roberts worked for S. S. Beman at Pullman, Illinois. In 1893, Roberts established his own office in Oak Park, and specialized in residential work.

A successful and popular architect, Roberts had the largest architectural office in Oak Park. In 1912 he moved his office to Chicago to concentrate on commercial work. Until 1923, when he formed a partnership with son, Elmer, Roberts practiced alone. Illness forced him into semi-retirement in 1926.

Thomas Eddy Tallmadge

b. April 24, 1876   Washington, D.C.
d. January 1, 1940   Arcola, Illinois

After graduating from M.I.T. with a B. S. in architecture, Tallmadge worked for D. H. Burnham until 1904 when he traveled in Europe after winning the Chicago Architectural Club Traveling Fellowship. In 1905 he and Vernon Watson formed a partnership that lasted until about 1936, after which Tallmadge practiced alone until his accidental death in 1940 in a railroad disaster.

Especially interested in the history of architecture, Tallmadge served for some years as professor of architectural history at the Armour Institute, and wrote three books on the subject: *The Story of Architecture in America; The Story of England's Architecture; Architecture in Old Chicago.* He was a member of several local and regional art societies and a member of the Architectural Commission for the Restoration of Colonial Williamsburg. At the Century of Progress exhibition he was architect of the Colonial Village.

John S. Van Bergen

b. October 2, 1885   Oak Park, Illinois
d. December 20, 1969   Santa Barbara, California

Following his graduation from Oak Park High School in 1905, Van Bergen spent about a year in California before returning to Chicago to work for Walter Griffin in 1907-8. After a three-month architectural course at the Chicago Technical College, Van Bergen went to work for Frank Lloyd Wright, remaining until his office closed, and after that he worked for architect William Drummond until June, 1911, when he passed the licensing examination. From 1911 until 1968 Van Bergen practiced alone, first at Oak Park, 1911-1917, then Highland Park, Illinois, 1920-1951, and later, Hawthorn Hills, Illinois, 1951-55, and Santa Barbara, California, 1955-69.

Vernon Spencer Watson

b. January 22, 1878   Chicago, Illinois
d. September 28, 1950   Berrien Springs, Michigan

Little is known about Watson's life. He studied architecture in a combined program offered by the Chicago Art and Armour Institutes during the late 1890's. He traveled in Europe at some time before 1900 and was working for D. H. Burnham in 1904 when he met Thomas Tallmadge who was to become his partner in 1905. Watson married shortly after the turn of the century and settled at Oak Park, living in a house he built for himself at 643 Fair Oaks Avenue (No. 55). After dissolving his partnership with Thomas Tallmadge in 1936, he retired to Berrien Springs, Michigan.

Charles E. White, Jr.

b. May 18, 1876   Lynn, Massachusetts
d. August 15, 1936   Oak Park, Illinois

Graduating from M.I.T. in 1895 with a B.S. in architecture, White found employment first with Swift & Co. in the planning of refrigeration in ships, and later as engineer and architect for the street railway companies in Ohio and Illinois. While in Rockford in 1901 he met and married Alice Roberts of Oak Park. In 1903 the couple settled in her home town, and White went to work for Frank Lloyd Wright. Leaving Wright early in 1905, White practiced alone until 1912, then with Charles Christie as White & Christie, and later with Bertram Weber, as White & Weber.

White wrote extensively for architectural journals and for ten years was on the staff of the *Ladies' Home Journal.* He also published two books on architecture, *Successful Houses and How to Build Them* and *The Bungalow Book.*

Frank Lloyd Wright

b. June 8, 1867   Richland Center, Wisconsin
d. April 9, 1959   Phoenix, Arizona

After studying engineering at the University of Wisconsin, Wright went to Chicago to find work as an architectural draftsman. His training was in the offices of Joseph Silsbee for one year, 1887-8, and with Adler & Sullivan for five years, 1888-93. In 1893 he established an independent practice which he pursued until his death in 1959. Oak Park was his home from 1887 to 1909, and six of his children were born here.

In 1931 he founded the Taliesin Fellowship to train architects partly at his estate in Wisconsin and partly at his winter home in Arizona. During his long career he also published a large number of books which include *Ausgefuhrte Bauten und Entwerfe; An Interpretation of Japanese Prints; Modern Architecture; The Nature of Materials; An Autobiography;* and *Genius and the Mobocracy.*

Wright was married three times, the first in 1889 to Catherine Tobin, then in 1922 to Mariam Noel, and last in 1928 to Olgivanna Lazovich, who succeeded him as head of the Taliesen Fellowship.

Beginning in 1900 and continuing to today, there has been a constant flow of articles and books about Wright's life, ideas, and architecture.

As summarized in an article appearing in The New Yorker, *"By almost universal acclaim, Frank Lloyd Wright is the most original architect the United States has ever produced and — what is more important — he is one of the most creative architectural geniuses of all time."*

Index